I0445578

Compiled by
Frater Lachesis Peyton
Tat Tvam Asi

SAKLAS
PUBLISHING

Neophyte Libri:

Official Neophyte Reading Syllabus

ISBN 979-8-9943016-1-6

Compilation © 2025 Saklas Publishing

A Note on this Series

The volume you hold is one of a series of companions to the work of the A∴A∴, the spiritual order established by Aleister Crowley and George Cecil Jones in 1907 and governed, in its inner life, by principles far older than either man. Each book in the series gathers into a single binding the official *libri*—the instructional texts—assigned to a particular grade of the Order.

The Probationer volume collects the writings that orient the newcomer and outline the first practices. The Neophyte volume presents the curriculum for those who have entered the Outer College in earnest. The Zelator volume carries the aspirant further, into deeper work with breath, will, memory, and the central scriptures of Thelema. Additional volumes, corresponding to higher grades, may follow in time.

The contents of each volume were determined by cross-referencing three primary sources. The first is Liber CLXXXV, *Liber Collegii Sancti*, the Class D document that sets out the official tasks, examinations, and oaths for every grade from Probationer to Adept. This text specifies which *libri* the aspirant at each grade is required to study, memorize, or master. The second is Liber CCVII, the *Syllabus of the Official Instructions of the* A∴A∴, which catalogues the full corpus of Order publications by class and number, with a description of each. Originally published in *The Equinox* I (10) in 1913 and subsequently revised, it serves as the authoritative index of what each liber is and where it stands in the system.

The third source is James A. Eshelman's *The Mystical and Magical System of the A∴A∴* (College of Thelema, 2000), a modern study that organizes the grade-by-grade curriculum into a practical working format, drawing on all available primary documents—including Liber XIII (*Graduum Montis Abiegni*), *One Star in Sight*, and the 1919 "Præmonstrance" and "Curriculum"—to clarify which texts belong to which grade when the official sources are ambiguous or incomplete. Where these three authorities agree, the assignment is straightforward. Where they differ, editorial judgment has been exercised, and such choices are noted where relevant.

These compilations contain only the *libri* themselves. Each grade of the A∴A∴ also prescribes a broader reading list that may include works by other authors—the *Tao Te Ching*, the *Dhammapada*, Patanjali's *Yoga Sutras*, the writings of David Hume, and others—as well as practices to be carried out under the guidance of a superior. Those external readings are not reproduced here. The present volumes are intended as a practical convenience: a way to keep the core instructional texts of a given grade together, in order, and in a readable form, so that the student may study them without hunting through scattered and sometimes unreliable sources.

The texts themselves carry a classification that the reader should understand.

Class A publications are writings received in a state of illumination, held to be supernally inspired, and not to be altered so much as by the style of a letter.

Class B writings are works of scholarship or informed exposition by individual adepts.

Class C is material suggested by A∴A∴ theory but not official.

Class D publications are the official rituals, instructions, and examination papers of the Order, setting out what is to be done and how.

Class E consists of public manifestos and other broadsheets. Some publications are composite, pertaining to more than one class.

The reader will find texts of several classes within each volume, and should approach them accordingly: a Class A text demands a different quality of attention than a Class D instruction on how to perform a ritual, though both are essential to the work.

Neophyte Libri

Official Neophyte Reading Syllabus

A∴A∴

Authored by Aleister Crowley
Compiled by Frater Lachesis Peyton

Contents

LIBER
LIBERI
VEL
LAPIDIS LAZULI

ADUMBRATIO KABBALÆ ÆGYPTIORUM

SUB FIGURÂ
VII

BEING THE VOLUNTARY EMANCIPATION OF A CERTAIN
EXEMPT ADEPT FROM HIS ADEPTSHIP. THESE ARE THE
BIRTH-WORDS OF A MASTER OF THE TEMPLE.

V

A∴A∴

Publication in Class A

The full knowledge of the interpretation of this book is
concealed from all, save only the Sixfold Star. The
Neophyte
must nevertheless acquire a copy and throughly acquaint
himself with the contents. He must commit one chapter
to memory.

PROLOGUE OF THE UNBORN

1. Into my loneliness comes—

2. The sound of a flute in dim groves that haunt the utmost hills.

3. Even from the brave river they reach to the edge of the wilderness.

4. And I behold Pan.

5. The snows are eternal, above—

6. And their perfume smokes upwards into the nostrils of the stars.

7. But what have I to do with these?

8. To me only the distant flute, the abiding vision of Pan.

9. On all sides Pan to the eye, to the ear;

10. The perfume of Pan pervading, the taste of him utterly filling my mouth, so that the tongue breaks forth into a weird and monstrous speech.

11. The embrace of him intense on every centre of pain and pleasure.

12. The sixth interior sense aflame with the inmost self of Him,

13. Myself flung down the precipice of being

14. Even to the abyss, annihilation.

15. An end to loneliness, as to all.

16. Pan! Pan! Io Pan! Io Pan!

I

1. My God, how I love Thee!

2. With the vehement appetite of a beast I hunt Thee through the Universe.

3. Thou art standing as it were upon a pinnacle at the edge of some fortified city. I am a white bird, and perch upon Thee.

4. Thou art My Lover: I see Thee as a nymph with her white limbs stretched by the spring.

5. She lies upon the moss; there is none other but she:

6. Art Thou not Pan?

7. I am He. Speak not, O my God! Let the work be accomplished in silence.

8. Let my cry of pain be crystallized into a little white fawn to run away into the forest.

9. Thou art a centaur, O my God, from the violet blossoms that crown Thee to the hoofs of the horse.

10. Thou art harder than tempered steel; there is no diamond beside Thee.

11. Did I not yield this body and soul?

12. I woo thee with a dagger drawn across my throat.

13. Let the spout of blood quench Thy blood-thirst, O my God!

14. Thou art a little white rabbit in the burrow Night.

15. I am greater than the fox and the hole.

16. Give me Thy kisses, O Lord God!

17. The lightning came and licked up the little flock of sheep.

18. There is a tongue and a flame; I see that trident walking over the sea.

19. A phúnix hath if for its head; below are two prongs. They spear the wicked.

20. I will spear Thee, O Thou little grey god, unless Thou beware!

21. From the grey to the gold; from the gold to that which is beyond the gold of Ophir.

22. My God! but I love Thee!

23. Why hast Thou whispered so ambiguous things? Wast thou afraid, O goat-hoofed One, O horned One, O pillar of lightning?

24. From the lightning fall pearls; from the pearls black specks of nothing.

25. I based all on one, one on naught.

26. Afloat in the Æthyr, O my God, my God!

27. O Thou great hooded sun of glory, cut off these eyelids!

28. Nature shall die out; she hideth me, closing mine eyelids with fear, she hideth me from My destruction, O Thou open eye.

29. O ever-weeping One!

30. Not Isis my mother, nor Osiris my self; but the incestuous Horus given over to Typhon, so may I be!

31. There thought; and thought is evil.

32. Pan! Pan! Io Pan! it is enough.

33. Fall not into death, O my soul! Think that death is the bed into which you are falling!

34. O how I love Thee, O my God! Especially is there a vehement parallel light from infinity, vilely diffracted in the haze of this mind.

35. I love Thee.

I love Thee.

I love Thee.

36. Thou art a beautiful thing whiter than a woman in the column of this vibration.

37. I shoot up vertically like an arrow, and become that Above.

38. But it is death, and the flame of the pyre.

39. Ascend in the flame of the pyre, O my soul! Thy God is like the cold emptiness of the utmost heaven, into which thou radiatest thy little light.

40. When Thou shalt know me, O empty God, my flame shall utterly expire in Thy great N.O.X.

41. What shalt Thou be, my God, when I have ceased to love Thee?

42. A worm, a nothing, a niddering knave!

43. But Oh! I love Thee.

44. I have thrown a million flowers from the basket of the Beyond at Thy feet, I have annointed Thee and Thy Staff with oil and blood and kisses.

45. I have kindled Thy marble into life—ay! into death.

46. I have been smitten with the reek of Thy mouth, that drinketh never wine but life.

47. How the dew of the Universe whitens the lips!

48. Ah! trickling flow of the stars of the mother Supernal, begone!

49. I am She that should come, the Virgin of all men.

50. I am a boy before Thee, O Thou satyr God.

51. Thou wilt inflict the punishment of pleasure— Now! Now! Now!

52. Io Pan! Io Pan! I love Thee. I love Thee.

53. O my God, spare me!

54. Now!

It is done! Death.

55. I cried aloud the word—and it was a mighty spell to bind the Invisible, an enchantment to unbind; yea, to unbind the bound.

II

1. O my God! use Thou me again, alway. For ever! For ever!

2. That which came fire from Thee cometh water from me; let therefore Thy Spirit lay hold on me, so that my right hand loose the lightning.

3. Travelling through space, I saw the onrush of two galaxies, butting each other and goring like bulls upon earth. I was afraid.

4. Thus they ceased fight, and turned upon me, and I was sorely crushed and torn.

5. I had rather have been trampled by the World-Elephant.

6. O my God! Thou art my little pet tortoise!

7. Yet thou sustainest the World-Elephant!

8. I creep under Thy carapace, like a lover into the bed of his beautiful; I creep in, and sit in Thine heart, as cubby and cosy as may be.

9. Thou shelterest me, that I hear not the trumpeting of that World-Elephant.

10. Thou art not worth an obol in the agora; yet Thou art not to be bought at the ransom of the whole Universe.

11. Thou art like a beautiful Nubian slave leaning her naked purple against the green pillars of marble that are above the bath.

12. Wine jets from her black nipples.

13. I drank wine awhile agone in the house of Pertinax. The cup-boy favoured me, and gave me of the right sweet Chian.

14. There was a Doric boy, skilled in feats of strength, an athlete. The full moon fled away angrily down the wrack.

Ah! but we laughed.

15. I was pernicious drunk, O my God! Yet Pertinax brought me to the bridal.

16. I have a crown of thorns for all my dower.

17. Thou art like a goat's horn from Astor, O Thou God of mine, gnarl'd and crook'd and devilish strong.

18. Colder than all the ice of all the glaciers of the Naked Mountain was the wine it poured for me.

19. A wild country and a waning moon.

Clouds scudding over the sky.

A circuit of pines, and of tall yews beyond.
Thou in the midst!

20. O all ye toads and cats rejoice! Ye slimy things, come hither!

21. Dance, dance to the Lord our God!

22. He is he! He is he! He is he!

23. Why should I go on?

24. Why? Why? comes the sudden cackle of a million imps of hell.

25. And the laughter runs.

26. But sickens not the Universe; but shakes not the stars.

27. God! how I love Thee!

28. I am walking in an asylum; all the men and women about me are insane.

29. Oh madness! madness! madness! desirable art thou!

30. But I love Thee, O God!

31. These men and women rave and howl; they froth out folly.

32. I begin to be afraid. I have no check; I am alone. Alone. Alone.

33. Think, O God, how I am happy in Thy love.

34. O marble Pan! O false leering face! I love Thy dark kisses, bloody and stinking! O marble Pan! Thy kisses are like sunlight on the blue Ægean; their blood is the blood of the sunset over Athens; their stink is like a garden of Roses of Macedonia.

35. I dreamt of sunset and roses and vines; Thou wast there, O my God, thou didst habit Thyself as an Athenian courtesan, and I loved Thee.

36. Thou art no dream, O Thou too beautiful alike for sleep and waking!

37. I disperse the inane folk of the earth; I walk alone with my little puppets in the garden.

38. I am Gargantuan great; yon galaxy is but the smoke-ring of mine incense.

39. Burn Thou strange herbs, O God!

40. Brew me a magic liquor, boys, with your glances.

41. The very soul is drunken.

42. Thou art drunken, O my God, upon my kisses.

43. The Universe reels; Thou hast looked upon it.

44. Twice, and all is done.

45. Come, O my God, and let us embrace!

46. Lazily, hungrily, ardently, patiently; so will I work.

47. There shall be an End.

48. O God! O God!

49. I am a fool to love Thee; Thou art cruel, Thou withholdest Thyself.

50. Come to me now! I love Thee! I love Thee!

51. O my darling, my darling—Kiss me! Kiss me! Ah! but again.

52. Sleep, take me! Death, take me! This life is too full; it pains, it slays, it suffices.

53. Let me go back into the world; yea, back into the world.

III

1. I was the priest of Ammon-Ra in the temple of Ammon-Ra at Thebai.

2. But Bacchus came singing with his troops of vine-clad girls, of girls in dark mantles; and Bacchus in the midst like a fawn!

3. God! how I ran out in my rage and scattered the chorus.

4. But in my temple stood Bacchus as the priest of Ammon-Ra.

5. Therefore I went wildly with the girls into Abyssinia; and there we abode and rejoiced.

6. Exceedingly; yea, in good sooth!

7. I will eat the ripe and the unripe fruit for the glory of Bacchus.

8. Terraces of ilex, and tiers of onyx and opal and sardonyx leading up to the cool green porch of malachite.

9. Within is a crystal shell, shaped like an oyster —O glory of Priapus! O beatitude of the Great Goddess!

10. Therein is a pearl.

11. O Pearl! thou hast come from the majesty of dread Ammon-Ra.

12. Then I the priest beheld a steady glitter in the heart of the pearl.

13. So bright we could not look. But behold! a blood-red rose upon a rood of glowing gold!

14. So I adored the God. Bacchus! thou art the lover of my God!

15. I who was priest of Ammon-Ra, who saw the Nile flow by for many moons, for many, many moons, am the young fawn of the grey land.

16. I will set up my dance in your conventicles, and my secret loves shall be sweet among you.

17. Thou shalt have a lover among the lords of the grey land.

18. This shall he bring unto thee, without which all is in vain; a man's life spilt for thy love upon Mine Altars.

19. Amen.

20. Let is be soon, O God, my God! I ache for Thee, I wander very lonely among the mad folk, in the grey land of desolation.

21. Thou shalt set up the abominable Thing of wickedness. Oh joy! to lay that corner-stone.

22. It shall stand erect upon the high mountain; only my God shall commune with it.

23. I will build it of a single ruby; it shall be seen from afar off.

24. Come! let us irritate the vessels of the earth: they shall distil strange wine.

25. It grows under my hand: it shall cover the whole heaven.

26. Thou art behind me: I scream with a mad joy.

27. Then said Ithuriel the strong; let Us also worship this invisible marvel!

28. So did they, and the archangels swept over the heaven.

29. Strange and mystic, like a yellow priest invoking mighty flights of great grey birds from the North, so do I stand and invoke Thee!

30. Let them obscure not the sun with their wings and their clamour!

31. Take away form and its following!

32. I am still.

33. Thou art like an osprey among the rice, I am the great red pelican in the sunset waters.

34. I am like a black eunuch; and Thou art the scimatar. I smite off the head of the light one, the breaker of bread and salt.

35. Yea! I smite—and the blood makes as it were a sunset on the lapis lazuli of the King's Bedchamber.

36. I smite. The whole world is broken up into a mighty wind, and a voice cries aloud in a tongue that men cannot speak.

37. I know that awful sound of primal joy; let us follow on the wings of the gale even unto the holy house of Hathor; let us offer the five jewels of the cow upon her altar!

38. Again the inhuman voice!

39. I rear my Titan bulk into the teeth of the gale, and I smite and prevail, and swing me out over the sea.

40. There is a strange pale God, a god of pain and deadly wickedness.

41. My own soul bites into itself, like a scorpion ringed with fire.

42. That pallid God with face averted, that God of subtlety and laughter, that young Doric God, him will I serve.

43. For the end thereof is torment unspeakable.

44. Better the loneliness of the great grey sea!

45. But ill befall the folk of the grey land, my God!

46. Let me smother them with my roses!

47. O Thou delicious God, smile sinister!

48. I pluck Thee, O my God, like a purple plum upon a sunny tree. How Thou dost melt in my mouth, Thou consecrated sugar of the Stars!

49. The world is all grey before mine eyes; it is like an old worn wine-skin.

50. All the wine of it is on these lips.

51. Thou hast begotten me upon a marble Statue, O my God!

52. The body is icy cold with the coldness of a million moons; it is harder than the adamant of eternity. How shall I come forth into the light?

53. Thou art He, O God! O my darling! my child! my plaything! Thou art like a cluster of maidens, like a multitude of swans upon the lake.

54. I feel the essence of softness.

55. I am hard and strong and male; but come Thou! I shall be soft and weak and feminine.

56. Thou shalt crush me in the wine-press of Thy love. My blood shall stain Thy fiery feet with litanies of Love in Anguish.

57. There shall be a new flower in the fields, a new vintage in the vinyards.

58. The bees shall gather a new honey; the poets shall sing a new song.

59. I shall gain the Pain of the Goat for my prize; and the God that sitteth upon the shoulders of Time shall drowse.

60. Then shall all this which is written be accomplished: yea, it shall be accomplished.

IV

1. I am like a maiden bathing in a clear pool of fresh water.

2. O my God! I see Thee dark and desirable, rising through the water as a golden smoke.

3. Thou art altogether golden, the hair and the eyebrows and the brilliant face; even into the finger-tips and toe-tips Thou art one rosy dream of gold.

4. Deep into Thine eyes that are golden my soul leaps, like an archangel menacing the sun.

5. My sword passes through and through Thee; crystalline moons ooze out of Thy beautiful body that is hidden behind the ovals of Thine eyes.

6. Deeper, ever deeper. I fall, even as the whole Universe falls down the abyss of Years.

7. For Eternity calls; the Overworld calls; the world of the Word is awaiting us.

8. Be done with speech, O God! Fasten the fangs of the hound Eternity in this my throat!

9. I am like a wounded bird flapping in circles.

10. Who knows where I shall fall?

11. O blessèd One! O God! O my devourer!

12. Let me fall, fall down, fall way, afar, alone!

13. Let me fall!

14. Nor is their any rest, Sweet Heart, save in the cradle of royal Bacchus, the thigh of the most Holy One.

15. There rest, under the canopy of night.

16. Uranus chid Eros; Marsyas chid Olympas; I chid my beautiful lover with his sunray mane; shall I not sing?

17. Shall not mine incantations bring around me the wonderful company of the wood-gods, their bodies glistening with the ointments of moonlight and honey and myrrh?

18. Worshipful are ye, O my lovers; let us forward to the dimmest hollow!

19. There we will feast upon mandrake and upon moly!

20. There the lovely One shall spread us his holy banquet. In the brown cakes of corn we shall taste the food of the world, and be strong.

21. In the ruddy and awful cup of death we shall drink the blood of the world, and be drunken!

22. Ohé! the song to Iao, the song to Iao!

23. Come, let us sing to thee, Iacchus invisible, Iacchus triumphant, Iacchus indicible!

24. Iacchus, O Iacchus, O Iacchus, be near us!

25. Then was the countenance of all time darkened, and the true light shone forth.

26. There was also a certain cry in an unknown tongue, whose stridency troubled the still waters of my soul, so that my mind and my body were healed of their disease, self-knowledge.

27. Yea, an angel troubled the waters.

28. This was the cry of Him: IIIOOOShBThIO-IOIIIIAMAMThIBI-II.

29. Nor did I sing this for a thousand times a night for a thousand nights before Thou camest, O my flaming God, and pierced me with Thy spear. Thy scarlet robe unfolded the whole heavens, so that the Gods said: All is burning: it is the end.

30. Also Thou didst set Thy lips to the wound and suck out a million eggs. And Thy mother sat upon them, and lo! stars and stars and ultimate Things whereof stars are the atoms.

31. Then I perceived Thee, O my God, sitting like a white cat upon the trellis-work of the arbour; and the hum of the spinning worlds was but Thy pleasure.

32. O white cat, the sparks fly from Thy fur! Thou dost crackle with splitting the worlds.

33. I have seen more of Thee in the white cat than I saw in the Vision of Æons.

34. In the boat of Ra did I travel, but I never found upon the visible Universe any being like unto Thee!

35. Thou wast like a winged white horse, and I raced Thee through eternity against the Lord of the Gods.

36. So still we race!

37. Thou wast like a flake of snow falling in the pine-clad woods.

38. In a moment Thou wast lost in a wilderness of the like and the unlike.

39. But I beheld the beautiful God at the back of the blizzard—and Thou wast He!

40. Also I read in a great Book.

41. On ancient skin was written in letters of gold: Verbum fit Verbum.

42. Also Vitriol and the hierophant's name V.V.V.V.V.

43. All this wheeled in fire, in star-fire, rare and far and utterly lonely—even as Thou and I, O desolate soul my God!

44. Yea, and the writing

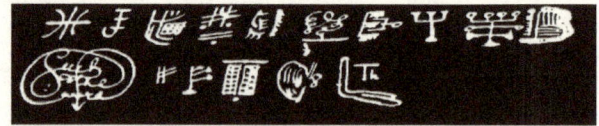

It is well.

This is the voice which shook the earth.

45. Eight times he cried aloud, and by eight and by eight shall I count Thy favours, Oh Thou Elevenfold God 418!

46. Yea, and by many more; by the ten in the twenty-two directions; even as the perpendicular of the Pyramid—so shall Thy favours be.

47. If I number them, they are One.

48. Excellent is Thy love, Oh Lord! Thou art revealed by the darkness, and he who gropeth in the horror of the groves shall haply catch Thee, even as a snake that seizeth on a little singing-bird.

49. I have caught Thee, O my soft thrush; I am like a hawk of mother-of-emerald; I catch Thee by instinct, though my eyes fail from Thy glory.

50. Yet they are but foolish folk yonder. I see them on the yellow sand, all clad in Tyrian purple.

51. They draw their shining God unto the land in nets; they build a fire to the Lord of Fire, and cry unhallowed words, even the dreadful curse Amri maratza, maratza, atman deona lastadza maratza maritza—marán!

52. Then do they cook the shining god, and gulp him whole.

53. These are evil folk, O beautiful boy! let us pass on to the Otherworld.

54. Let us make ourselves into a pleasant bait, into a seductive shape.

55. I will be like a splendid naked woman with ivory breasts and golden nipples; my whole body shall be like the milk of the stars. I will be lustrous and Greek, a courtesan of Delos, of the unstable Isle.

56. Thou shalt be like a little red worm on a hook.

57. But thou and I will catch our fish alike.

58. Then wilt thou be a shining fish with golden back and silver belly: I will be like a violent beautiful man, stronger than two score bulls, a man of the West bearing a great sack of precious jewels upon a staff that is greater than the axis of the all.

59. And the fish shall be sacrificed to Thee and the strong man crucified for Me, and Thou and I will

kiss, and atone for the wrong of the Beginning; yea,
for the wrong of the beginning.

V

1. O my beautiful God! I swim in Thy heart like a trout in the mountain torrent.

2. I leap from pool to pool in my joy; I am goodly with brown and gold and silver.

3. Why, I am lovelier than the russet autumn woods at the first snowfall.

4. And the crystal cave of my thought is lovelier than I.

5. Only one fish-hook can draw me out; it is a woman kneeling by the bank of the stream. It is she that pours the bright dew over herself, and into the sand so that the river gushes forth.

6. There is a bird on yonder myrtle; only the song of that bird can draw me out of the pool of Thy heart, O my God!

7. Who is this Neapolitan boy that laughs in his happiness? His lover is the mighty crater of the Mountain of Fire. I saw his charred limbs borne down the slopes in a stealthy tongue of liquid stone.

8. And Oh! the chirp of the cicada!

9. I remember the days when I was cacique in Mexico.

10. O my God, wast Thou then as now my beautiful lover?

11. Was my boyhood then as now Thy toy, Thy joy?

12. Verily, I remember those iron days.

13. I remember how we drenched the bitter lakes with our torrent of gold; how we sank the treasurable image in the crater of Citlalteptl.

14. How the good flame lifted us even unto the lowlands, setting us down in the impenetrable forest.

15. Yea, Thou wast a strange scarlet bird with a bill of gold. I was Thy mate in the forests of the lowland; and ever we heard from afar the shrill chant of mutilated priests and the insane clamour of the Sacrifice of Maidens.

16. There was a weird winged God that told us of his wisdom.

17. We attained to be starry grains of gold dust in the sands of a slow river.

18. Yea, and that river was the river of space and time also.

19. We parted thence; ever to the smaller, ever to the greater, until now, O sweet God, we are ourselves, the same.

20. O God of mine, Thou art like a little white goat with lightning in his horns!

21. I love Thee, I love Thee.

22. Every breath, every word, every thought, every deed is an act of love with Thee.

23. The beat of my heart is the pendulum of love.

24. The songs of me are the soft sighs.

25. The thoughts of me are very rapture.

26. And my deeds are the myriads of Thy children, the stars and the atoms.

27. Let there be nothing!

28. Let all things drop into this ocean of love!

29. Be this devotion a potent spell to exorcise the demons of the Five!

30. Ah God, all is gone! Thou dost consummate Thy rapture. Falútli! Falútli!

31. There is a solemnity of the silence. There is no more voice at all.

32. So shall it be unto the end. We who were dust shall never fall away into the dust.

33. So shall it be.

34. Then, O my God, the breath of the Garden of Spices. All these have a savour averse.

35. The cone is cut with an infinite ray; the curve of the hyperbolic life springs into being.

36. Farther and farther we float; yet we are still. It is the chain of systems that is falling away from us.

37. First falls the silly world; the world of the old grey land.

38. Falls it unthinkingly far, with its sorrowful bearded face presiding over it; it fades to silence and woe.

39. We to silence and bliss, and the face is the laughing face of Eros.

40. Smiling we greet him with the secret signs.

41. He leads us into the Inverted Palace.

42. There is the Heart of Blood, a pyramid reaching its apex down below the Wrong of the Beginning.

43. Bury me unto Thy Glory, O beloved, O princely lover of this harlot maiden, within the Secretest Chamber of the Palace.

44. It is done quickly; yea, the seal is set upon the vault.

45. There is one that shall avail to open it.

46. Nor by memory, nor by imagination, nor by prayer, nor by fasting, nor by scourging, nor by drugs, nor by ritual, nor by meditation; only by passive love shall he avail.

47. He shall await the sword of the Beloved and bare his throat for the first stroke.

48. Then shall his blood leap out and write me runes in the sky; yea, write me runes in the sky.

VI

1. Thou wast a priestess, O my God, among the Druids; and we knew the powers of the oak.

2. We made us a temple of stones in the shape of the Universe, even as thou didst wear openly and I concealed.

3. There we performed many wonderful things by midnight.

4. By the waning moon did we work.

5. Over the plain came the atrocious cry of wolves.

6. We answered; we hunted with the pack.

7. We came even unto the new Chapel and Thou didst bear away the Holy Graal beneath Thy Druid vestments.

8. Secretly and by stealth did we drink of the informing sacrament.

9. Then a terrible disease seized upon the folk of the grey land; and we rejoiced.

10. O my God, disguise Thy glory!

11. Come as a thief, and let us steal away the Sacraments!

12. In our groves, in our cloistral cells, in our honeycomb of happiness, let us drink, let us drink!

13. It is the wine that tinges everything with the true tincture of infallible gold.

14. There are deep secrets in these songs. It is not enough to hear the bird; to enjoy song he must be the bird.

15. I am the bird, and Thou art my song, O my glorious galloping God!

16. Thou reinest in the stars; thou drivest the constellations seven abreast through the circus of Nothingness.

17. Thou Gladiator God!

18. I play upon mine harp; Thou fightest the beasts and the flames.

19. Thou takest Thy joy in the music, and I in the fighting.

20. Thou and I are beloved of the Emperor.

21. See! he has summoned us to the Imperial dais.

> The night falls; it is a great orgy of worship and bliss.

22. The night falls like a spangled cloak from the shoulders of a prince upon a slave.

23. He rises a free man!

24. Cast thou, O prophet, the cloak upon these slaves!

25. A great night, and scarce fires therein; but freedom for the slave that its glory shall encompass.

26. So also I went down into the great sad city.

27. There dead Messalina bartered her crown for poison from the dead Locusta; there stood Caligula, and smote the seas of forgetfulness.

28. Who was Thou, O Cæsar, that Thou knewest God in an horse?

29. For lo! we beheld the White Horse of the Saxon engraven upon the earth; and we beheld the Horses of the Sea that flame about the old grey land, and the foam from their nostrils enlightens us!

30. Ah! but I love thee, God!

31. Thou art like a moon upon the ice-world.

32. Thou art like the dawn of the utmost snows upon the burnt-up flats of the tiger's land.

33. By silence and by speech do I worship Thee.

34. But all is in vain.

35. Only Thy silence and Thy speech that worship me avail.

36. Wail, O ye folk of the grey land, for we have drunk your wine, and left ye but the bitter dregs.

37. Yet from these we will distil ye a liquor beyond the nectar of the Gods.

38. There is value in our tincture for a world of Spice and gold.

39. For our red powder of projection is beyond all possibilities.

40. There are few men; there are enough.

41. We shall be full of cup-bearers, and the wine is not stinted.

42. O dear my God! what a feast Thou hast provided.

43. Behold the lights and the flowers and the maidens!

44. Taste of the wines and the cates and the splendid meats!

45. Breathe in perfumes and the clouds of little gods like wood-nymphs that inhabit the nostrils!

46. Feel with your whole body the glorious smoothness of the marble coolth and the generous warmth of the sun and the slaves!

47. Let the Invisible inform all the devouring Light of its disruptive vigour!

48. Yea! all the world is split apart, as an old grey tree by the lightning!

49. Come, O ye gods, and let us feast.

50. Thou, O my darling, O my ceaseless Sparrow-God, my delight, my desire, my deceiver, come Thou and chirp at my right hand!

51. This was the tale of the memory of Al A'in the priest; yea, of Al A'in the priest.

VII

1. By the burning of the incense was the Word revealed, and by the distant drug.

2. O meal and honey and oil! O beautiful flag of the moon, that she hangs out in the centre of bliss.

3. These loosen the swathings of the corpse; these unbind the feet of Osiris, so that the flaming God may rage through the firmament with his fantastic spear.

4. But of pure black marble is the sorry statue, and the changeless pain of the eyes is bitter to the blind.

5. We understand the rapture of that shaken marble, torn by the throes of the crowned child, the golden rod of the golden God.

6. We know why all is hidden in the stone, within the coffin, within the mighty sepulchre, and we too answer Olalám! Imál! Tutúlu! as it is written in the ancient book.

7. Three words of that book are as life to a new Æon; no god has read the whole.

8. But Thou and I, O God, have written it page by page.

9. Ours is the elevenfold reading of the Elevenfold word.

10. These seven letters together make seven diverse words; each word is divine, and seven sentences are hidden therein.

11. Thou art the Word, O my darling, my lord, my master!

12. O come to me, mix the fire and the water, all shall dissolve.

13. I await Thee in sleeping, in waking. I invoke Thee no more; for Thou art in me, O Thou who hast made me a beautiful instrument tuned to Thy rapture.

14. Yet art Thou ever apart, even as I.

15. I remember a certain holy day in the dusk of the year, in the dusk of the Equinox of Osiris, when first I beheld Thee visibly; when first the dreadful issue was fought out; when the Ibis-headed One charmed away the strife.

16. I remember Thy first kiss, even as a maiden should. Nor in the dark byways was there another: Thy kisses abide.

17. There is none other beside Thee in the whole Universe of Love.

18. My God, I love Thee, O Thou goat with gilded horns!

19. Thou beautiful bull of Apis! Thou beautiful serpent of Apep! Thou beautiful child of the Pregnant Goddess!

20. Thou hast stirred in Thy sleep, O ancient sorrow of years! Thou hast raised Thine head to strike, and all is dissolved into the Abyss of Glory.

21. An end to the letters of the words! An end to the sevenfold speech.

22. Resolve me the wonder of it all into the figure of a gaunt swift camel striding over the sand.

23. Lonely is he, and abominable; yet hath he gained the crown.

24. Oh rejoice! rejoice!

25. My God! O my God! I am but a speck in the star-dust of ages; I am the Master of the Secret of Things.

26. I am the Revealer and the Preparer. Mine is the Sword—and the Mitre and the Wingèd Wand!

27. I am the Initiator and the Destroyer. Mine is the Globe—and the Bennu Bird and the Lotus of Isis my daughter!

28. I am the One beyond these all; and I bear the symbols of the mighty darkness.

29. There shall be a sigil as of a vast black brooding ocean of death and the central blaze of darkness, radiating its night upon all.

30. It shall swallow up that lesser darkness.

31. But in that profound who shall answer: What is?

32. Not I.

33. Not Thou, O God!

34. Come, let us no more reason together; let us enjoy! Let us be ourselves, silent, unique, apart.

35. O lonely woods of the world! In what recesses will ye hide our love?

36. The forest of the spears of the Most High is called Night, and Hades, and the Day of Wrath; but I am His captain, and I bear His cup.

37. Fear me not with my spearmen! They shall slay the demons with their petty prongs. Ye shall be free.

38. Ah, slaves! ye will not—ye know not how to will.

39. Yet the music of my spears shall be a song of freedom.

40. A great bird shall sweep from the Abyss of Joy, and bear ye away to be my cup-bearers.

41. Come, O my God, in one last rapture let us attain to the Union with the Many!

42. In the silence of Things, in the Night of Forces, beyond the accursèd domain of the Three, let us enjoy our love!

43. My darling! My darling! away, away beyond the Assembly and the Law and the Enlightenment unto an Anarchy of Solitude and Darkness!

44. For even thus must we veil the brilliance of our Self.

45. My darling! My darling!

46. O my God, but the love in Me burst over the bonds of Space and Time; my love is spilt among them that love not love.

47. My wine is poured out for them that never tasted wine.

48. The fumes thereof shall intoxicate them and the vigour of my love shall breed mighty children from their maidens.

49. Yea! without draught, without embrace:—and the Voice answered Yea! these things shall be.

50. Then I sought a Word for Myself; nay, for myself.

51. And the Word came: O Thou! it is well. Heed naught! I love Thee! I love Thee!

52. Therefore had I faith unto the end of all; yea, unto the end of all.

LIBER
XIII
VEL
GRADUUM
MONTIS
ABIEGNI

A SYLLABUS
OF THE STEPS
UPON THE
PATH

V

A∴A∴

Publication in Class D

Issued by Order:
D.D.S. 7° = 4° Præmonstrator
O.S.V. 6° = 5° Imperator
N.S.F. 5° = 6° Cancellarius

Let not the failure and the pain turn aside the worshippers. The foundations of the pyramid were hewn in the living rock ere sunset; did the king weep at dawn that the crown of the pyramid was as yet unquarried in the distant land?

There was also an humming-bird that spake unto the horned cerastes, and prayed him for poison. And the great snake of Khem the Holy One, the royal Uræus serpent, answered him and said:

I sailed over the sky of Nu in the car called Millions-of-Years, and I saw not any creature upon Seb that was equal to me. The venom of my fang is the inheritance of my father, and of my father's father; and how shall I give it unto thee? Live thou and thy children as I and my fathers have lived, even unto an hundred millions of generations, and it may be that the mercy of the Mighty Ones may bestow upon thy children a drop of the poison of eld.

Then the humming-bird was afflicted in his spirit, and he flew unto the flowers, and it was as if naught had been spoken between them. Yet in a little while a serpent struck him that he died.

But an Ibis that meditated upon the bank of Nile the beautiful god listened and heard. And he laid aside his Ibis ways, and became as a serpent, saying Peradventure in an hundred millions of millions of generations of my children, they shall attain to a drop of the poison of the fang of the Exalted One.

And behold! ere the moon waxed thrice he became an Uræus serpent, and the poison of the fang was established in him and his seed even for ever and for ever.

—*Liber LXV, ch. V. vv. 51-56.*

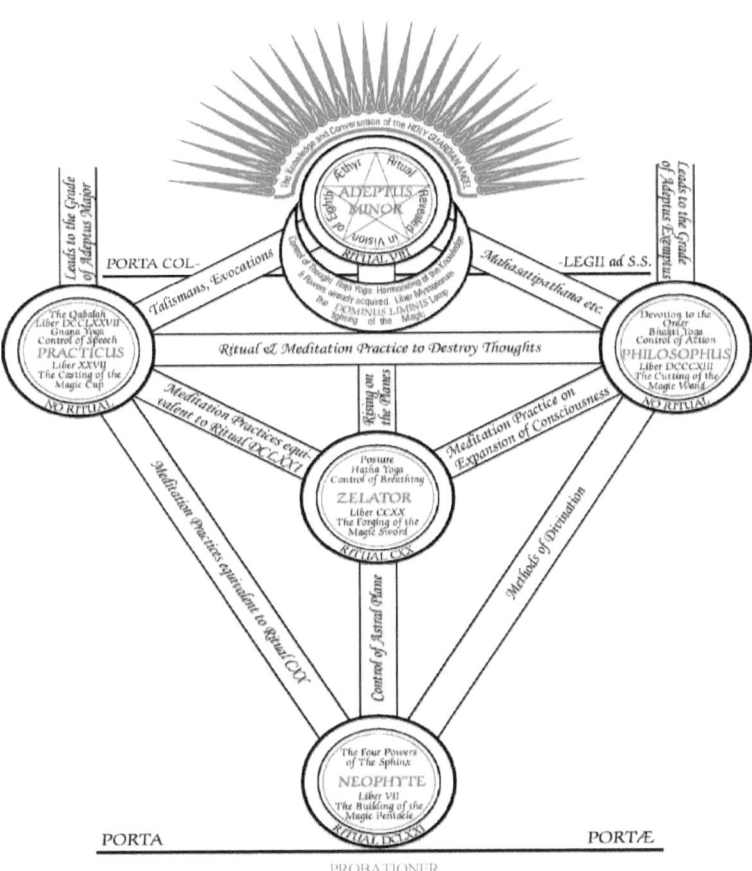

1. The Probationer. His duties are laid down in Paper A, Class D. Being without, they are vague and general. He receives Liber LXI and LXV.

[Certain Probationers are admitted after six months or more to Ritual XXVIII.]

At the end of the Probation he passes Ritual DCLXXI which constitutes him a Neophyte.

2. The Neophyte. His duties are laid down in Paper B, Class D. He receives Liber VII.

Examination in Liber O, Caps I.–IV., Theoretical and Practical.

Examination in The Four Powers of the Sphinx. Practical.

Four Tests are set.

Further, he builds up the magic Pentacle.

Finally he passes Ritual CXX, which constitutes him a Zelator.

3. The Zelator. His duties are laid down in Paper C, Class D. He receives Liber CCXX, XXVII, and DCCCXIII.

Examinations in Posture and Control of Breath (see Equinox vol. I No. 1). Practical.

Further, he is given two meditation-practices corresponding to the two rituals DCLXXI and CXX.

(Examination is only in the knowledge of, and some little practical acquaintance with, these meditations. The complete results, if attained, would confer a much higher grade.)

Further, he forges the Magic Sword.

No ritual admits to the grade of Practicus, which is conferred by authority when the task of the Zelator is accomplished.

4. The Practicus. His duties are laid down in Paper D, Class D.

Instruction and Examination in the Qabalah and Liber 777.

Instruction in Philosophical Meditation (Gnana-Yoga).*

Examination in some one mode of divination: e.g. Geomancy, Astrology, the Tarot. Theoretical.

He is given a meditation-practice on Expansion of Consciousness.

He is given a meditation-practice in the destruction of thoughts.

Instruction and examination in Control of Speech. Practical.

Further, he casts the magic Cup.

No ritual admits to the grade of Philosophus, which is conferred by authority when the Task of the Practicus is accomplished.

5. The Philosophus. His duties are laid down in Paper E, Class D.

He practices Devotion to the Order. Instruction and Examination in Methods of Meditation by Devotion (Bhakti-Yoga).

Instruction and Examination in Construction and Consecration of Talismans, and in Evocation.
˙ Theoretical and Practical.

Examination in Rising on the Planes (Liber O, Caps V., VI.). Practical.

He is given a meditation-practice on the Senses, and the Sheaths of the Self, and the Practice called mahāsatipatthāna.

(See The Sword of Song, "Science and Buddhism.")

Instruction and Examination in Control of Action.

Further, he cuts the Magic Wand.

Finally, the Title of Dominus Liminis is conferred upon him.

He is given meditation-practices on the Control of Thought, and is instructed in Raja-Yoga.

He receives Liber Mysteriorum and obtains a perfect understanding of the Formulæ of Initiation.

He meditates upon the diverse knowledge and power that he has acquired, and harmonises it perfectly.

Finally, he lights the Magic Lamp.

At last, Ritual VIII admits him to the grade of Adeptus Minor.

All these instructions will be issued openly in The Equinox in due course, where this has not already been done.

6. The Adeptus Minor. His duty is laid down in Paper G, Class D.

It is to follow out the instruction given in the Eighth Æthyr for the attainment of the Knowledge and Conversation of the Holy Guardian Angel.

[NOTE. This is in truth the sole task; the others are useful only as adjuvants to and preparations for the One Work. Moreover, once this task has been accomplished, there is no more need of human help or instruction; for by this alone may the highest attainment be reached.

All these grades are indeed but convenient landmarks, not necessarily significant. A person who had attained them all might be immeasurably the inferior of one who had attained none of them; it is Spiritual Experience alone that counts in Result; the rest is but Method.

Yet it is important to possess knowledge and power, provided that it be devoted wholly to that One Work.]

Ritual XXVIII

THE CEREMONY OF THE SEVEN HOLY KINGS

(Probationers, who are idle or luxurious, shall be given a task suitable to their natures. If they refuse the task from laziness or from a feeling that they have more important business (as their Neophyte may judge) then may V.V.V.V.V. 8°=3° himself inform them with much deference that they are now fitted for admission to the Mystery of the Seven Holy Kings.)

(The Temple is arranged as shewn in the attached illustration [missing in this copy].)

The God of the first Throne hath robes of Deep Blue; second—Violet; 3rd.—Scarlet; 4th.—Orange; 5th.—Green; 6th.—Pale Yellow; 7th.—Bright Blue. The other officers are the Hegemon, clad in white & masked in white, & in his hand is the Phoenix Wand of the Planets; & the Hiereus, masked in black & robed in black, in his hands are the Scourge & Crook. The Candidate, well fed & joyful, clad in the Robe of a Probationer, & crowned with laurel, is led by the Hegemon (his Neophyte) into the Hall. Taken to the altar, on which burns a small fire of odorous wood, cedar or sandal or lignum aloes, he is made to kneel thereat, & the Black officer comes forward threatening him with his scourge & saith:

H: Who art Thou?

Hg., for Cand.: I am the Aspirant to the Sacred & Sublime Order of A∴A∴ & I seek the aid of Osiris.

(Note: This ceremony can be adapted for working by two officers, the Hegemon assuming each time a different coloured cloak, & the appropriate God-form. But it is most desirable that the full complement of Nine should assist.)

"Hail unto thee, Osiris, triumphant, Lord of Amennta, Lord of Enenet! Hail unto thee, all glorious sun of mercy & justice, upon whose head is the golden crown of light that is invisible to men! Hail unto thee, hail unto thee, sole light in our darkness! Hail unto thee through whom alone (...) may attain unto the Brotherhood Immortal. Deign to guide this aspirant in the straight path, & let him not fall into the way of those who err." (There is no answer).

"Let us arise, & seek Osiris." (They come to the First Throne.)

SATURN

"Welcome, welcome, welcome, for thou art chosen, O thou that hast aspired to the Brotherhood Immortal. Aspiration is strength, & I give thee of my bounty: Peace & plenty & contentment & good health & length of days. All these hast thou won by virtue of that single aspiration. But beware of the black shadow at my side, for he shall put ice against thy heart; he shall constrict thy whole being; he shall bring thee to sorrow & poverty & premature old age if thou so much as lift thine eyes unto his face. Place therefore thine head upon my knees, that I may put mine hands upon thine head, & bless thee with my blessings." (He does so.) "Welcome wast thou, & thou shalt be welcome to my brethren. Pass thou on." (They reach the Second Throne.)

JUPITER

"Welcome, welcome, welcome, for thou art chosen,
O thou that hast aspired to the Brotherhood
Immortal. Aspiration is strength, & I give thee of my
bounty: Authority, & the respect of men, &
distinction & praise & veneration. All these hast
thou won by virtue of that single aspiration. But
beware of the black shadow at my side, for he shall
cast thee down, & thou shalt be despised of all men,
& thy power shall be broken if thou so much as lift
thine eyes unto his face. Place therefore thine head
upon my knees, that I may put mine hands upon
thine head, & bless thee with my blessings." (He
does so.) "Welcome wast thou, & thou shalt be
welcome to my brethren. Pass thou on." (They reach
the Third Throne.)

MARS

"Welcome, welcome, welcome, for thou art chosen,
O thou that hast aspired to the Brotherhood
Immortal. Aspiration is strength, & I give thee of my
bounty: Courage & energy & force; conquest &
dominion. All these hast thou won by virtue of that
single aspiration. But beware of the black shadow at
my side, for he shall burn thee as with fire, & all that
thou hast shalt thou lose. And in thy battles shalt
thou be overcome, & thou shalt be broken & ground
into dust if thou so much as lift thine eyes unto his
face. Place therefore thine head upon my knees, that
I may put mine hands upon thine head, & bless thee
with my blessings." (He does so.) "Welcome wast
thou, & thou shalt be welcome to my brethren. Pass
thou on." (They reach the Fourth Throne.)

SUN

"Welcome, welcome, welcome, for thou art chosen, O thou that hast aspired to the Brotherhood Immortal. Aspiration is strength, & I give thee of my bounty: Fame & jollity, & a life fair & open; glory & harmony shall be thy servants, & victory shall wait upon thee as an handmaid. All these hast thou won by virtue of that single Aspiration. But beware of the black shadow at my side, for he shall drive thee from the life of men, so that thou hidest in dens & caverns from the light, & thy name shall be lost, & thou shalt suddenly be slain if thou so much as lift thine eyes unto his face. Place therefore thine head upon my knees, that I may put mine hands upon thine head, & bless thee with my blessings." (He does so.) "Welcome wast thou, & thou shalt be welcome to my brethren. Pass thou on." (They reach the Fifth Throne.)

VENUS

"Welcome, welcome, welcome, for thou art chosen, O thou that hast aspired to the Brotherhood Immortal. Aspiration is strength, & I give thee of my bounty: Love & beauty & true happiness, ease & abundance. All these hast thou won by virtue of that single aspiration. But beware of the black shadow at my side for he shall destroy love in thee, & all thy beauty shall be blasted, & no word of kindness shalt thou ever hear again if thou so much as lift thine eyes unto his face. Place therefore thine head upon my knees, that I may put mine hands upon thine head, & bless thee with my blessings." (He does so.) "Welcome wast thou, & thou shalt be welcome to my brethren. Pass thou on." (They reach the Sixth Throne.)

MERCURY

"Welcome, welcome, welcome, for thou art chosen, O thou that hast aspired to the Brotherhood Immortal. Aspiration is strength, & I give thee of my bounty: Learning, & eloquence, & the power to heal the ills of men. All these hast thou won by virtue of that single aspiration. But beware of the black shadow at my side, for a thief shall come upon thee & despoil thee; & thou shalt have no more knowledge, & with disease thy body shall dissolve away if thou so much as lift thine eyes unto his face. Place therefore thine head upon my knees, that I may put mine hands upon thine head, & bless thee with my blessings." (He does so.) "Welcome wast thou, & thou shalt be welcome to my brethren. Pass thou on." (They reach the Seventh Throne.)

MOON

"Welcome, welcome, welcome, for thou art chosen, O thou that hast aspired to the Brotherhood Immortal. Aspiration is strength, & I give thee of my bounty: Purity & clearness of vision, & all the harvest of delight. All these hast thou won by virtue of that single aspiration. But beware of the black shadow at my side, for he shall darken thine eyes, & thou shalt waste away, & thou shalt go a-cold, & thou shalt suddenly be slain if thou so much as lift thine eyes unto his face. Place therefore thine head upon my knees, that I may put mine hands upon thine head, & bless thee with my blessings." (He does so.) "Welcome wast thou to me, as thou wast welcome to my brethren; thou didst but lift up thine hand in aspiration to the Brotherhood Immortal, & thou hast swept the seven chords of the celestial harp. Pass thou on."

They go back, not to the altar, but to the little door of the temple, within which is a dark dungeon. The

Hegemon thrusts him furiously into this with hand & foot, all crying aloud "Osiris is a black god." There he must remain for seven hours.

(If at any point previous in the ritual he should say "I ask not these blessings; I seek Osiris. What saith yon silent dark one?" or words of similar purport, the Hegemon answers, removing the hoodwink once and for all, "Verily, thou sayest well; know that Osiris is a black God, & the straight way unto the Sacred & Sublime Order lieth not through the green pastures & beside still waters. But in the Valley of the Shadow of Death, His crook & scourge shall avail thee.

"Take them therefore & fold thine arms upon thy breast; ascend with me the seven steps of the Throne."

The Aspirant then does so, standing between the officers. The Fourth Throne is removed to leave a passage. The Seven Kings rush upon him & belabor him with their weapons; but he makes his way & they fall one by one; the Seventh upon the Second step, the Sixth upon the Third, the Fifth upon the Fourth, the Fourth upon the Fifth, the Third upon the Sixth, the Second upon the Seventh & the First at the Foot of the Throne. The Aspirant passes over their bodies & takes his seat. They then, each from his place, adore him while the two officers support him on either side, & the Hierophant addresses him:

"Frater _____ this day have I symbolically placed thee in the seat of a Brother of the A∴A∴. See to it that thy life truly reflect this gradual conquest of the Powers of the Seven, & never forget that thy path is the path of Osiris,—& that Osiris is a black God."

(They then conduct him from the temple.)

(After the seven hours are past, the Aspirant is rescued by Osiris, the black officer, in the words already given, omitting "Verily thou sayest well" & using a sterner tone for the beginning of the speech. The ceremony then proceeds as before.)

THE COMPLETE SYMBOL OF THE TAROT

THE COMPLETE SYMBOL OF THE TAROT

A DESCRIPTION OF
THE CARDS OF THE TAROT

H R U
THE GREAT ANGEL

is

set over the operations of the Secret Wisdom

A XAI Ω

The First and the Last

"WHAT thou seest, write in a book, and send it unto the Seven Abodes which be in Aushiah."

"And I saw in the Right Hand of Him that Sate upon the Throne a Book, sealed with Seven Seals."

"Who is worthy to open the book, and to loose the Seals thereof?"

S.Y.M.B.O.L.A.

THE FRONTISPIECE

CONSISTS of a Crux Ansata, which is a form of the Rosy Cross. One arm is scarlet, with the symbols of Leo and the Wand in emerald green.

Another is blue with Eagle and Cup in orange.

A third is yellow, with Aquarius and Dagger in violet.

The last is in the four colours of Malkuth, with Pentacle and Taurus in black.

Ring is white, having at the top the Name of the Great Angel H R U H U A; below cross-bar are Pentagrams, one enclosing Sol and the other enclosing Luna.

The whole space in the ring contains the Rose of 22 Petals bearing the Names of the 22 Keys. In the centre a white circle, and a red cross of four equal arms.

About the whole symbol are the words L.I.F.E. B.I.O.S. V.I.T.A., and the letters— T. A. P. O., Tarot.

THE TITLES OF THE SYMBOLS

1. The Ace of Wands is called the Root of the Powers of Fire.

2. The Ace of Cups is called the Root of the Powers of Water.

3. The Ace of Swords is called the Root of the Powers of Air.

4. The Ace of Pentacles is called the Root of the Powers of Earth.

5. The Knight of Wands is "The Lord of the Flame and Lighting: the King of the Spirits of Fire."

6. The Queen of Wands is "The Queen of the Thrones of Flame."

7. The King of Wands is "The Prince of the Chariot of Fire."

8. The Knave of Wands is "The Princess of the Shining Flame: the Rose of the Palace of Fire."

9. The Knight of Cups is "The Lord of the Waves and the Waters: the King of the Hosts of the Sea."

10. The Queen of Cups is "The Queen of the Thrones of the Waters."

11. The King of Cups is "The Prince of the Chariot of the Waters."

12. The Knave of Cups is "The Princess of the Waters: the Lotus of the Palace of the Floods."

13. The Knight of Swords is "The Lord of the Wind and the Breezes: the King of the Spirits of Air."

14. The Queen of Swords is "The Queen of the Thrones of Air."

15. The King of Swords is "The Prince of the Chariot of the Winds."

16. The Knave of Swords is "The Princess of the Rushing Winds: the Lotus of the Palace of Air."

17. The Knight of Pentacles is "The Lord of the Wide and Fertile Land: the King of the Spirits of Earth."

18. The Queen of Pentacles is "The Queen of the Thrones of Earth."

19. The King of Pentacles is "The Prince of the Chariot of Earth."

20. The Knave of Pentacles is "The Princess of the Echoing Hills: the Rose of the Palace of Earth."

THE THIRTY-SIX DECAN CARDS

NO.	CARD	LORD OF	DECAN	IN
21.	5 of Wands	Strife	♄	♌
22.	6 of Wands	Victory	♃	♌
23.	7 of Wands	Valour	♂	♌
24.	8 of Pentacles	Prudence	☉	♍
25.	9 of Pentacles	Material Gain	♀	♍
26.	10 of Pentacles	Wealth	☿	♍
27.	2 of Swords	Peace Restored	☽	♎
28.	3 of Swords	Sorrow	♄	♎
29.	4 of Swords	Rest from Strife	♃	♎
30.	5 of Cups	Loss in Pleasure	♂	♏
31.	6 of Cups	Pleasure	☉	♏
32.	7 of Cups	Illusionary Success	♀	♏
33.	8 of Wands	Swiftness	☿	♐
34.	9 of Wands	Great Strength	☽	♐
35.	10 of Wands	Oppression	♄	♐
36.	2 of Pentacles	Harmonious Change	♃	♑
37.	3 of Pentacles	Material Works	♂	♑
38.	4 of Pentacles	Earthly Power	☉	♑
39.	5 of Swords	Defeat	♀	♒
40.	6 of Swords	Earned Success	☿	♒
41.	7 of Swords	Unstable Effort	☽	♒
42.	8 of Cups	Abandoned Success	♄	♓
43.	9 of Cups	Material Happiness	♃	♓
44.	10 of Cups	Perfected Success	♂	♓
45.	2 of Wands	Dominion	♂	♈
46.	3 of Wands	Established Strength	☉	♈
47.	4 of Wands	Perfected Work	♀	♈
48.	5 of Pentacles	Material Trouble	☿	♉
49.	6 of Pentacles	Material Success	☽	♉
50.	7 of Pentacles	Success Unfulfilled	♄	♉
51.	8 of Swords	Shortened Force	♃	♊
52.	9 of Swords	Despair and Cruelty	♂	♊
53.	10 of Swords	Ruin	☉	♊
54.	2 of Cups	Love	♀	♋
55.	3 of Cups	Abundance	☿	♋
56.	4 of Cups	Blended Pleasure	☽	♋

THE TWENTY-TWO KEYS OF THE BOOK

57. 0. The Foolish Man — The Spirit of Αιθηρ — א — Air

58. 1. The Magician — The Magus of Power — ב — Mercury

59. 2. The High Priestess — The Priestess of the Silver Star — ג — Moon

60. 3. The Empress — The Daughter of the Mighty Ones — ד — Venus

61. 4. The Emperor — Son of the Morning, chief among the Mighty — ה — Aries

62. 5. The Hierophant — The Magus of the Eternal — ו — Taurus

63. 6. The Lovers — The Children of the Voice; the Oracles of the Mighty Gods — ז — Gemini

64. 7. The Chariot — The Child of the Powers of the Waters; the Lord of the Triumph of Light — ח — Cancer

65. 11. Fortitude — The Daughter of the Flaming Sword — ט — Leo

66. 9. The Hermit — The Magus of the Voice of Power, the Prophet of the Eternal — י — Virgo

67. 10. The Wheel of Fate — The Lord of the Forces of Life — כ — Jupiter

68. 8. Justice — The Daughter of the Lords of Truth: the Ruler of the Balance — ל — Libra

69. 12. The Hanged Man — The Spirit of the Mighty Waters — מ — Water

70. 13. Death — The Child of the Great Transformers: the Lord of the Gates of Death — נ — Scorpio

71. 14. Temperance — The Daughter of the Reconcilers: the Bringer-Forth of Life — ס — Sagittarius

72. 15. The Devil — The Lord of the Gates of Matter: the Child of the Forces of Time — ע — Capricorn

73. 16. The Blasted Tower — The Lord of the Hosts of the Mighty — פ — Mars

74. 17. The Star — The Daughter of the Firmament, the Dweller between the Waters — צ — Aquarius

75. 18. The Moon — The Ruler of Flux and Reflux: the Child of the Sons of the Mighty — ק — Pisces

76. 19. The Sun — The Lord of the Fire of the World — ר — Sun

77. 20. The Judgment — The Spirit of the Primal Fire — ש — Fire

78. 21. The Universe — The Great One of the Night of Time — ת — Saturn/Earth

Such are the Titles of the Abodes or Atouts of Thooth;

of the Mansions of the House of my FATHER.

The Descriptions of the Seventy-eight Symbols of this Book; together with their meanings

OF THE ACES

FIRST in order and importance are the Four Aces, representing the Force of the Spirit, acting in, and binding together, the Four Scales of each Element: and answering to the Dominion of the Letters of the Name in the Kether of each. They represent the Radical Forces.

The Four Aces are said to be placed on the North Pole of the Universe wherein they revolve, governing its revolution; and ruling as the connecting link between Yetzirah and the Material Plane or Universe.

I
THE ROOT OF THE POWERS OF FIRE
Ace of Wands

A WHITE Radiating Angelic Hand, issuing from clouds, and grasping a heavy club, which has three branches in the colours, and with the sigils, of the scales. The Right-and Left-hand branches end respectively in three Flames, and the Centre one in four Flames: thus yielding Ten: the Number of the Sephiroth. Two-and-twenty leaping Flames, or Yodh, surround it, answering to the Paths; of these, three fall below the Right branch for Aleph, Mem, and Shin, seven above the Central branch for the double letters; and between it and that of the Right twelve: six above and six below about the Left-hand branch. The whole is a great and flaming Torch. It symbolizes Force—strength, rush, vigour, energy, and it governs, according to its nature, various works and questions.

It implies Natural, as opposed to Invoked, Force.

II

THE ROOT OF THE POWERS OF THE WATERS

Ace of Cups or Chalices

A WHITE Radiant Angelic Hand, issuing from clouds, and supporting on the palm thereof a cup, resembling that of the Stolistes.

From it rises a fountain of clear and glistening water: and sprays falling on all sides into clear calm water below, in which grow Lotuses and Water-lilies. The great Letter of the Supernal Mother is traced in the spray of the Fountain.

It symbolizes Fertility—productiveness, beauty, pleasure, happiness, etc.

III

THE ROOT OF THE POWERS OF THE AIR

Ace of Swords

A WHITE Radiating Angelic Hand, issuing from clouds, and grasping the hilt of a sword, which supports a White Radiant Celestial Crown; from which depend, on the right, the olive branch of Peace; and on the left, the palm branch of suffering.

Six Vaus fall from its point. It symbolizes "Invoked," as contrasted with Natural Force: for it is the Invocation of the Sword. Raised upward, it invokes the Divine crown of Spiritual Brightness, but reversed it is the Invocation of Demonic Force; and becomes a fearfully evil symbol. It represents, therefore, very great power for good or evil, but invoked; and it also represents whirling Force, and strength through trouble. It is the affirmation of Justice upholding Divine Authority; and it may become the Sword of Wrath, Punishment, and Affliction.

IV
THE ROOT OF THE POWERS OF THE EARTH
Ace of Pentacles

A WHITE Radiant Angelic Hand, holding a branch of a Rose Tree, whereon is a large Pentacle, formed of Five concentric circles. The Innermost Circle is white, charged with a red Greek Cross. From this White Centre, Twelve Rays, also white, issue: these terminate at the circumference, making the whole something like an Astrological figure of the Heavens.

It is surmounted by a small circle, above which is a large white Maltese Cross, and with two white wings.

Four Crosses and two buds are shewn. The Hand issueth from the Clouds as in the other three cases.

It represents materiality in all senses, good and evil: and is, therefore, in a sense, illusionary: it shows material gain, labour, power, wealth, etc.

THE SIXTEEN COURT, OR ROYAL CARDS

The Four Kings

THE Four Kings, or "Figures mounted on steeds," represent the Yodh forces of the Name in each Suit: the Radix, Father and commencement of Material Forces, a force in which all the others are implied, and of which they form the development and completion. A force swift and violent in its action, but whose effect soon passes away, and therefore symbolized by a Figure on a Steed riding swiftly, and clothed in complete Armour.

Therefore is the knowledge of the scale of the King so necessary for the commencement of all magical working.

The Four Queens

are seated upon Thrones; representing the Forces of the Hé of the Name in each suit; the Mother and bringer-forth of Material Forces: a force which develops and realizes that of the King: a force steady and unshaken, but not rapid, though enduring. It is therefore symbolized by a Figure seated upon a Throne: but also clothed in Armour.

The Four Princes

These Princes are Figures seated in Chariots, and thus borne forward. They represent the Vau Forces of the Name in each suit: the Mighty Son of the King and Queen, who realizes the influence of both scales of Force. A Prince, the son of a King and Queen, yet a Prince of Princes, and a King of Kings: an Emperor whose effect is at once rapid (though not so swift as that of the Queen) and enduring. It is, therefore, symbolized by a Figure borne in a Chariot, and clothed in Armour. Yet is his power vain and illusionary, unless set in Motion by his Father and Mother.

The Four Princesses

are the Knaves of the Tarot Pack; The Four Princesses or figures of Amazons, standing firmly of themselves: neither riding upon Horses, nor seated upon Thrones, nor borne in Chariots. They represent the forces of the Hé final of the Name in each suit, completing the Influences of the other scales: The mighty and potent daughter of a King and Queen: a Princess powerful and terrible: a Queen of Queens—an Empress—whose effect combines those of the King, Queen, and Prince, at once violent and permanent; therefore symbolized by a Figure standing firmly by itself, only partially draped, and having but little Armour; yet her power existeth not, save by reason of the others: and then indeed it is mighty and terrible materially, and is the Throne of the Forces of the Spirit.

Woe unto whomsoever shall make war upon her, when thus established!

THE SPHERES OF INFLUENCE OF THE COURT CARDS OF THE TAROT PACK

THE Princesses rule the Four Parts of the Celestial Heavens which lie around the North Pole, and above the respective Cherubic Signs of the Zodiac, and they form the Thrones of the Powers of the Four Aces.

The twelve cards, the Four Kings, Queens and Princes rule the dominion of the Celestial Heavens, between the realm of the Four Princesses and the Zodiac, as is hereafter shewn. And they, as it were, link together the signs.

V

THE LORD OF THE FLAME AND THE LIGHTNING; THE KING OF THE SPIRITS OF FIRE

Knight of Wands

A WINGED Warrior riding upon a black horse with flaming mane and tail: the horse itself is not winged. The rider wears a winged helmet (like the old Scandinavian and Gaulish helmet) with a Rayed Crown, a corslet of scale-mail and buskins of the same, and a flowing scarlet mantle. Above his helmet, upon his cuirass, and on the shoulder-pieces and buskins, he wears as a crest a winged black horse's head. He grasps a club with flaming ends, somewhat similar to that in the symbol of the Ace of Wands, but not so heavy, and also the sigil of his scale is shown; beneath the rushing feet of his steed are waving flames and fire. He is active—generous— fierce—sudden—impetuous.

If ill dignified, he is evil-minded—cruel—bigoted— brutal.

He rules the celestial heavens from above the Twentieth Degree of Scorpio to the First Two Decans of Sagittarius: and this includes a part of the Constellation Hercules. (Hercules is always represented with a Club.)

Fire of Fire

King of the Salamanders.

[Note that the Kings are now called Knights, and the Princes are now called Kings. This is unfortunate, and leads to confusion; the Princes may be called Emperors without harm. Remember only that the horsed figures refer to the Yod of Tetragrammaton, the charioted figures to the Vau.]

VI

THE QUEEN OF THE THRONES OF FLAME

Queen of Wands

A CROWNED Queen with long red-golden hair, seated upon a Throne, with steady flames beneath. She wears a corslet and buskins of scale-mail, which latter her robe discloses. Her arms are almost bare. On cuirass and buskins are leopard's heads winged, and the same symbol surmounteth her crown. At her side is a couchant leopard on which her hands rest. She bears a long wand with a very heavy conical head. The face is beautiful and resolute.

Adaptability, steady force applied to an object, steady rule, great attractive power, power of command, yet liked notwithstanding. Kind and generous when not opposed.

If ill dignified, obstinate, revengeful, domineering, tyrannical, and apt to turn against another without a cause.

She rules the heavens from above the last Decan of Pisces to above the 20° of Aries: including thus a part of Andromeda.

Water of Fire

Queen of the Salamanders.

VII
THE PRINCE OF THE CHARIOT OF FIRE
King of Wands

A KINGLY Figure with a golden, winged crown, seated on a chariot. He has large white wings. One wheel of his chariot is shewn. He wears corslet and buskins of scale armour decorated with a winged lion's head, which symbol also surmounts his crown. His chariot is drawn by a lion. His arms are bare, save for the shoulder-pieces of the corslet, and he bears a torch or fire-wand, somewhat similar to that of the Zelator Adeptus Minor. Beneath the chariot are flames, some waved, some salient.

Swift, strong, hasty; rather violent, yet just and generous; noble and scorning meanness.

If ill dignified—cruel, intolerant, prejudiced and ill natured.

He rules the heavens from above the last Decan of Cancer to the second Decan of Leo; hence he includes most of Leo Minor.

Air of Fire

Prince and Emperor of Salamanders.

VIII

THE PRINCESS OF THE SHINING FLAME; THE ROSE OF THE PALACE OF FIRE

Knave of Wands

A VERY strong and beautiful woman with flowing red-gold hair, attired like an Amazon. Her shoulders, arms, bosom and knees are bare. She wears a short kilt reaching to the knee. Round her waist is a broad belt of scale-mail; narrow at the sides; broader in front and back; and having a winged tiger's head in front. She wears a Corinthian-shaped helmet and crown with a long plume. It also is surmounted by a tiger's head, and the same symbol forms the buckle of her scale-mail buskins. A mantle lined with tiger's skin falls back from her shoulders. Her right hand rests on a small golden or brazen altar ornamented with ram's heads and with Flames of Fire leaping from it. Her left hand leans on a long and heavy club, swelling at the lower end, where the sigil is placed; and it has flames of fire leaping from it the whole way down; but the flames are ascending. This club or torch is much longer than that carried by the King or Queen. Beneath her firmly placed feet are leaping Flames of Fire.

Brilliance, courage, beauty, force, sudden in anger or love, desire of power, enthusiasm, revenge.

If ill dignified, she is superficial, theatrical, cruel, unstable, domineering.

She rules the heavens over one quadrant of the portion around the North Pole.

Earth of Fire

Princess and Empress of the Salamanders.

Throne of the Ace of Wands.

IX

THE LORD OF THE WAVES AND THE WATERS; THE KING OF THE HOSTS OF THE SEA

Knight of Cups

A BEAUTIFUL, winged, youthful Warrior with flying hair, riding upon a white horse, which latter is not winged. His general equipment is similar to that of the Knight of Wands, but upon his helmet, cuirass and buskins is a peacock with opened wings. He holds a cup in his hand, bearing the sigil of the scale. Beneath his horse's feet is the sea. From the cup issues a crab.

Graceful, poetic, Venusian, indolent, but enthusiastic if roused.

Ill dignified, he is sensual, idle and untruthful.

He rules the heavens from above 20° of Aquarius to 20° of Pisces, thus including the greater part of Pegasus.

Fire of Water

King of Undines and Nymphs.

X

THE QUEEN OF THE THRONES OF THE WATERS

Queen of Cups

A VERY beautiful fair woman like a crowned Queen, seated upon a throne, beneath which is flowing water wherein Lotuses are seen. Her general dress is similar to that of the Queen of Wands, but upon her crown, cuirass and buskins is seen an Ibis with opened wings, and beside her is the same bird, whereon her hand rests. She holds a cup, wherefrom a crayfish issues. Her face is dreamy. She holds a lotus in the hand upon the Ibis.

She is imaginative, poetic, kind, yet not willing to take much trouble for another. Coquettish, good-natured and underneath a dreamy appearance. Imagination stronger than feeling. Very much affected by other influences, and therefore more dependent upon dignity than most symbols.

She rules from 20° Gemini to 20° Cancer.

Water of Water

Queen of Nymphs or Undines.

XI

THE PRINCE OF THE CHARIOT OF THE WATERS

King of Cups

A WINGED Kingly Figure with winged crown seated in a chariot drawn by an eagle. On the wheel is the symbol of a scorpion. The eagle is borne as a crest on his crown, cuirass and buskins. General attire like King of Wands. Beneath his chariot is the calm and stagnant water of a lake. His armour resembles feathers more than scales. He holds in one hand a lotus, and in the other a cup, charged with the sigil of his scale. A serpent issues from the cup, and has its head tending down to the waters of the lake.

He is subtle, violent, crafty and artistic; a fierce nature with calm exterior. Powerful for good or evil but more attracted by the evil if allied with apparent Power or Wisdom.

If ill dignified, he is intensely evil and merciless.

He rules from 20° Libra to 20° Scorpio.

Air of Water

Prince and Emperor of Nymphs or Undines.

XII

THE PRINCESS OF THE WATERS; THE LOTUS OF THE PALACE OF THE FLOODS

Knave of Cups

A BEAUTIFUL Amazon-like figure, softer in nature than the Princess of Wands. Her attire is similar. She stands on a sea with foaming spray. Away to her right a Dolphin. She wears as a crest a swan with opening wings. She bears in one hand a lotus, and in the other an open cup from which a turtle issues.

Her mantle is lined with swansdown, and is of thin floating material.

Sweetness, poetry, gentleness and kindness. Imaginative, dreamy, at times indolent, yet courageous if roused.

When ill dignified she is selfish and luxurious.

She rules a quadrant of the heavens around Kether.

Earth of Water

Princess and Empress of the Nymphs or Undines.

Throne of the Ace of Cups.

XIII

THE LORD OF THE WINDS AND THE BREEZES: THE KING OF THE SPIRITS OF AIR

Knight of Swords

A WINGED Warrior with crowned Winged Helmet, mounted upon a brown steed. His general equipment is as that of the Knight of Wands, but he wears as a crest a winged six-pointed star, similar to those represented on the heads of Castor and Pollux the Dioscuri, the twins Gemini (a part of which constellation is included in his rule). He holds a drawn sword with the sigil of his scale upon its pommel. Beneath his horse's feet are dark-driving stratus clouds.

He is active, clever, subtle, fierce, delicate, courageous, skilful, but inclined to domineer. Also to overvalue small things, unless well dignified.

If ill dignified, deceitful, tyrannical and crafty.

Rules from 20° Taurus to 20° Gemini.

Fire of Air

King of the Sylphs and Sylphides.

XIV
THE QUEEN OF THE THRONES OF AIR
Queen of Swords

A GRACEFUL woman with wavy, curling hair, like a
Queen seated upon a Throne and crowned. Beneath
the Throne are grey cumulus clouds. Her general
attire is as that of the Queen of Wands, but she
wears as a crest a winged child's head. A drawn
sword in one hand, and in the other a large,
bearded, newly severed head of a man.

Intensely perceptive, keen observation, subtle, quick
and confident: often persevering, accurate in
superficial things, graceful, fond of dancing and
balancing.

If ill dignified, cruel, sly, deceitful, unreliable,
though with a good exterior.

Rules from 20° Virgo to 20° Libra.

Water of Air

Queen of the Sylphs and Sylphides.

XV
THE PRINCE OF THE CHARIOT OF THE WINDS
King of Swords

A WINGED King with Winged Crown, seated in a
chariot drawn by Arch Fays, represented as winged
youths very slightly dressed, with butterfly wings:
heads encircled by a fillet with a pentagram thereon:

and holding wands surmounted by pentagrams, the same butterfly wings on their feet and fillets. General equipment as the King of Wands: but he bears as a crest a winged angelic head with a pentagram on the brows. Beneath the chariot are grey nimbus clouds. His hair long and waving in serpentine whirls, and whorl figures compose the scales of his armour. A drawn sword in one hand; a sickle in the other. With the sword he rules, with the sickle he slays.

Full of ideas and thoughts and designs, distrustful, suspicious, firm in friendship and enmity; careful, observant, slow, over-cautious, symbolizes A and Ω; he slays as fast as he creates.

If ill dignified: harsh, malicious, plotting; obstinate, yet hesitating; unreliable.

Rules from 20° Capricorn to 20° Aquarius.

Air of Air

Prince and Emperor of the Sylphs and Sylphides.

XVI

THE PRINCESS OF THE RUSHING WINDS: THE LOTUS OF THE PALACE OF AIR

Knave of Swords

AN AMAZON figure with waving hair, slighter than the Rose of the Palace of Fire. Her attire is similar. The Feet seem springy, giving the idea of swiftness. Weight changing from one foot to another and body swinging around. She is a mixture of Minerva and Diana: her mantle resembles the Ægis of Minerva. She wears as a crest the head of the Medusa with serpent hair. She holds a sword in one hand; and the other rests upon a small silver altar with grey smoke (no fire) ascending from it. Beneath her feet are white clouds.

Wisdom, strength, acuteness; subtlety in material things: grace and dexterity.

If ill dignified, she is frivolous and cunning.

She rules a quadrant of the heavens around Kether.

Earth of Air

Princess and Empress of the Sylphs and Sylphides.

Throne of the Ace of Swords.

XVII
THE LORD OF THE WIDE AND FERTILE LAND; THE KING OF THE SPIRITS OF EARTH

Knight of Pentacles

A DARK Winged Warrior with winged and crowned helmet: mounted on a light brown horse. Equipment as the Knight of Wands.

The winged head of a stag or antelope as a crest. Beneath the horse's feet is fertile land with ripened corn. In one hand he bears a sceptre surmounted by a hexagram: in the other a Pentacle like that of the Zelator Adeptus Minor.

Unless very well dignified he is heavy, dull, and material. Laborious, clever, and patient in material matters.

If ill dignified, he is avaricious, grasping, dull, jealous; not very courageous, unless assisted by other symbols.

Rules from above 20° of Leo to 20° of Virgo.

Fire of Earth

King of Gnomes.

XVIII
THE QUEEN OF THE THRONES OF EARTH
Queen of Pentacles

A WOMAN of beautiful face with dark hair; seated upon a throne, beneath which is dark sandy earth. One side of her face is light, the other dark; and her symbolism is best represented in profile. Her attire is similar to that of the Queen of Wands: but she bears a winged goat's head as a crest. A goat is by her side. In one hand she bears a sceptre surmounted by a cube, and in the other an orb of gold.

She is impetuous, kind; timid, rather charming; great-hearted; intelligent, melancholy; truthful, yet of many moods.

If ill dignified she is undecided, capricious, changeable, foolish.

She rules from 20° Sagittarius to 20° Capricorn.

Water of Earth

The Queen of Gnomes.

XIX
THE PRINCE OF THE CHARIOT OF EARTH
King of Pentacles

A WINGED Kingly Figure seated in a chariot drawn by a bull. He bears as a crest the symbol of the head of the winged bull. Beneath the chariot is land, with many flowers. In the one hand he bears an orb of gold held downwards, and in the other a sceptre surmounted by an orb and cross.

Increase of matter. Increases good or evil, solidifies; practically applies things. Steady; reliable.

If ill dignified he is selfish, animal and material: stupid. In either case slow to anger, but furious if roused.

Rules from 20° Aries to 20° Taurus.

Air of Earth

Prince and Emperor of the Gnomes.

XX

PRINCESS OF THE ECHOING HILLS: ROSE OF THE PALACE OF EARTH

Knave of Pentacles

A STRONG and beautiful Amazon figure with rich brown hair, standing on grass or flowers. A grove of trees near her. Her form suggests Hebe, Ceres, and Proserpine. She bears a winged ram's head as a crest: and wears a mantle of sheepskin. In one hand she carries a sceptre with a circular disk: in the other a Pentacle similar to that of the Ace of Pentacles.

She is generous, kind, diligent, benevolent, careful, courageous, persevering, pitiful.

If ill dignified she is wasteful and prodigal. She rules over one quadrant of the heavens around the North Pole of the Ecliptic.

Earth of Earth

Princess and Empress of the Gnomes.

Throne of the Ace of Pentacles.

OF THE THIRTY-SIX DECANS

HERE follow the descriptions of the smaller cards of the four suits, thirty-six in number, answering unto the thirty-six Decans of the Zodiac.

XXI

THE LORD OF STRIFE

Five of Wands

TWO White Radiant Angelic Hands issuant per nubes dexter and sinister. They are clasped together in the grip of the First Order, i.e. the four fingers of each right hand crooked into each other, the thumbs meeting above; and they hold, at the same time, by their centres, five wands or torches which are similar unto the wands of a Zelator Adeptus Minor. One wand is upright in the middle; the others cross each other. Flames leap from the point of junction. Above the middle wand is the sign Saturn, and below is that of Leo: thus representing the Decanate. Violent strife and boldness, rashness, cruelty, violence, lust, desire, prodigality and generosity; depending on whether the card is well or ill dignified.

Geburah of ' (Quarrelling and fighting).

This Decan hath its beginning from the Royal Star of Leo: and unto it are allotted the two great Angels of the Schemhamphorash והויה and ילילי.

[The proper meaning of the small cards is to be found by making thorough meditation and harmony

76

between these four symbols of each card. It will be seen that this is how the meanings have been done; but the advanced student can go beyond this rude working.]

XXII
THE LORD OF VICTORY
Six of Wands

TWO hands in grip as the last, holding six wands crossed three and three. Flames issue from the point of junction. Above and below are short wands with flames issuing, surmounted respectively by the symbols of Jupiter and Leo, representing the Decan.

Victory after strife: Love: pleasure gained by labour: carefulness, sociability and avoiding of strife, yet victory therein: also insolence, and pride of riches and success, etc. The whole dependent on the dignity.

Tiphareth of י (Gain).

Hereunto are allotted the great Angels סיטאל and עלמיה of the Schemhamphorash.

XXIII
THE LORD OF VALOUR
Seven of Wands

TWO hands holding by grip six wands, three crossed. A third hand issuing from a cloud at the lower part of the card, holding an upright wand which passes between the others. Flames leap from the point of junction. Above and below the central wand are the symbols of Mars and Leo, representing the Decan.

Possible victory, depending on the energy and courage exercised; valour; opposition, obstacles and difficulties, yet courage to meet them; quarrelling, ignorance, pretence, and wrangling, and threatening; also victory in small and unimportant things: and influence upon subordinates.

Netzach of ' (Opposition, yet courage).

Therein rule the two great Angels מהשיה and ללהאל of the Schemhamphorash.

XXIV
THE LORD OF PRUDENCE
Eight of Pentacles

A WHITE Radiating Angelic Hand, issuing from a cloud, and grasping a branch of a rose tree, with four white roses thereon, which touch only the four lowermost Pentacles. No rosebuds even, but only leaves, touch the four uppermost disks. All the Pentacles are similar to that of the Ace, but without the Maltese cross and wings. They are arranged like the geomantic figure Populus. Above and below them are the symbols Sun and Virgo for the Decan.

Over-careful in small things at the expense of great: "Penny wise and pound foolish": gain of ready money in small sums; mean; avaricious; industrious; cultivation of land; hoarding, lacking in enterprise.

Hod of ה (Skill: prudence: cunning).

Therein rule those mighty Angels אכאיה and כהתאל.

XXV
THE LORD OF MATERIAL GAIN
Nine of Pentacles

A WHITE Radiating Angelic Hand, holding a rose branch with nine white roses, each of which touches a Pentacle. The Pentacles are arranged thus: three rows of three. And there are rosebuds on the branches as well as flowers. Venus and Virgo above and below.

Complete realization of material gain, good, riches; inheritance; covetous; treasuring of goods; and sometimes theft and knavery. The whole according to dignity.

Yesod of ה (Inheritance, much increase of goods).

Herein those mighty Angels הזיאל and אלדיה have rule and dominion.

XXVI
THE LORD OF WEALTH
Ten of Pentacles

AN Angelic Hand, holding by the lower extremity a branch whose roses touch all the Pentacles. No buds, however, are shewn. The symbols of Mercury and Virgo are above and below.

The Pentacles are arranged in the form of the Tree of Life.

Completion of material gain and fortune; but nothing beyond: as it were, at the very pinnacle of success. Old age, slothfulness; great wealth, yet sometimes loss in part; heaviness; dullness of mind, yet clever and prosperous in money transactions.

Malkuth of ה (Riches and wealth).

Herein are לויה and ההעיה set over this Decan as Angel Rulers.

XXVII

THE LORD OF PEACE RESTORED

Two of Swords or Pikes

Two crossed swords, like the air dagger of a Z.A.M.,
each held by a White Radiant Angelic Hand. Upon
the point where the two cross is a rose of five petals,
emitting white rays. At the top and bottom of the
card are two small daggers, supporting respectively
the symbol Moon thus, and Libra representing the
Decanate.

Contradictory characters in the same nature,
strength through suffering; pleasure after pain.
Sacrifice and trouble, yet strength arising
therefrom, symbolized by the position of the rose, as
though the pain itself had brought forth beauty.
Arrangement, peace restored; truce; truth and
untruth; sorrow and sympathy. Aid to the weak;
arrangement; justice, unselfishness; also a tendency
to repetition of affronts on being pardoned; injury
when meaning well; given to petitions; also a want
of tact, and asking question of little moment;
talkative.

Chokmah of ı. Quarrel made up, yet still some
tension in relations: actions sometimes selfish,
sometimes unselfish.

Herein rule the Great Angels יזלאל and מנהאל.

XXVIII

THE LORD OF SORROW

Three of Swords or Spears

THREE White Radiating Angelic Hands, issuing from
clouds, and holding three swords upright (as though
the central sword had struck apart the two others,

80

which were crossed in the preceding symbol): the central sword cuts asunder the rose of five petals, which in the previous symbol grew at the junction of the swords; its petals are falling, and no white rays issue from it.

Above and below the central sword are the symbols of Saturn and Libra.

Disruption, interruption, separation, quarrelling; sowing of discord and strife, mischief-making, sorrow and tears; yet mirth in Platonic pleasures; singing, faithfulness in promises, honesty in money transactions, selfish and dissipated, yet sometimes generous: deceitful in words and repetitions; the whole according to dignity.

Binah of ı (Unhappiness, sorrow, and tears).

Herein rule the Great Angels הריאל and הקמיה as Lords of the Decan.

XXIX
THE LORD OF REST FROM STRIFE
Four of Swords

TWO White Radiating Angelic Hands, each holding two swords; which four cross in the centre. The rose of five petals with white radiations is reinstated on the point of their intersection. Above and below, on the points of two small daggers, are Jupiter and Libra, representing the Decanate.

Rest from sorrow; yet after and through it. Peace from and after war. Relaxation of anxiety. Quietness, rest, ease and plenty, yet after struggle. Goods of this life; abundance; modified by dignity as is usual.

Chesed of ו (Convalescence, recovery from sickness; change for the better).

Herein do לויה and כליאל bear rule.

XXX

THE LORD OF LOSS IN PLEASURE

Five of Cups or Chalices

A WHITE Radiating Angelic Hand, holding lotuses or water-lilies, of which the flowers are falling right and left. Leaves only, and no buds, surmount them. These lotus stems ascend between the cups in the manner of a fountain, but no water flows therefrom; neither is there water in any of the cups, which are somewhat of the shape of the magical instrument of the Zelator Adeptus Minor.

Above and below are the symbols of Mars and Scorpio for the Decan.

Death, or end of pleasure: disappointment, sorrow and loss in those things from which pleasure is expected. Sadness, treachery, deceit; ill-will, detraction; charity and kindness ill requited; all kinds of anxieties and troubles from unsuspected and unexpected sources.

Geburah of ה (Disappointment in love, marriage broken off, unkindness of a friend; loss of friendship).

Herein rule לוויה and פהליה.

XXXI

THE LORD OF PLEASURE

Six of Chalices

AN Angelic Hand, as before, holds a group of stems of water-lilies or lotuses, from which six flowers bend, one over each cup. From these flowers a white glistening water flows into the cups as from a fountain, but they are not yet full. Above and below are Sun and Scorpio referring to the Decan.

Commencement of steady increase, gain and pleasure; but commencement only. Also affront, detection, knowledge, and in some instances contention and strife arising from unwarranted self-assertion and vanity. Sometimes thankless and presumptuous; sometimes amiable and patient. According to dignity as usual.

Tiphareth of ה (Beginning of wish, happiness, success, or enjoyment).

Therein rule נלכאל and ייאל.

XXXII
THE LORD OF ILLUSIONARY SUCCESS
Seven of Chalices

THE seven cups are arranged as two descending triangles above a point: a hand, as usual, holds lotus stems which arise from the central lower cup. The hand is above this cup and below the middle one. With the exception of the central lower cup, each is overhung by a lotus flower, but no water falls from these into any of the cups, which are all quite empty. Above and below are the symbols of the Decanate Venus and Scorpio.

Possible victory, but neutralized by the supineness of the person: illusionary success, deception in the moment of apparent victory. Lying, error, promises unfulfilled. Drunkenness, wrath, vanity. Lust, fornication, violence against women, selfish dissipation, deception in love and friendship. Often success gained, but not followed up. Modified as usual by dignity.

Netzach of ה (Lying, promises unfulfilled; illusion, deception, error; slight success at outset, not retained).

Herein the Angels מלהאל and חהויה rule.

XXXIII

THE LORD OF SWIFTNESS

Eight of Wands or Torches

FOUR White Radiating Angelic Hands (two proceeding from each side) issuant from clouds; clasped in two pairs in the centre with the grip of the First Order. They hold eight wands, crossed four with four. Flames issue from the point of junction. Surmounting the small wands with flames issuing down them, and placed in the centre at the top and bottom of the card respectively, are the symbols of Mercury and Sagittarius for the Decan.

Too much force applied too suddenly. Very rapid rush, but quickly passed and expended. Violent, but not lasting. Swiftness, rapidity, courage, boldness, confidence, freedom, warfare, violence; love of open air, field-sports, gardens and meadows. Generous, subtle, eloquent, yet somewhat untrustworthy; rapacious, insolent, oppressive. Theft and robbery. According to dignity.

Hod of י (Hasty communications and messages; swiftness).

Therein rule the Angels נתהיה and האאיה.

XXXIV

THE LORD OF GREAT STRENGTH

Nine of Wands or Torches

FOUR hands, as in the previous symbol, holding eight wands crossed four and four; but a fifth hand at the foot of the card holds another wand upright, which traverses the point of junction with the others: flames leap herefrom. Above and below are the symbols Moon and Sagittarius.

Tremendous and steady force that cannot be shaken. Herculean strength, yet sometimes scientifically applied. Great success, but with strife and energy. Victory, preceded by apprehension and fear. Health good, and recovery not in doubt. Generous, questioning and curious; fond of external appearances: intractable, obstinate.

Yesod of ' (Strength, power, health, recovery from sickness).

Herein rule the Angels ירתאל and שאהיה.

XXXV

THE LORD OF OPPRESSION

Ten of Wands

FOUR hands holding eight wands crossed as before. A fifth hand holding two wands upright, which traverses the junction of the others. Flames issuant. Saturn and Sagittarius.

Cruel and overbearing force and energy, but applied only to material and selfish ends. Sometimes shows failure in a matter, and the opposition too strong to be controlled; arising from the person's too great selfishness at the beginning. Ill-will, levity, lying, malice, slander, envy, obstinacy; swiftness in evil and deceit, if ill dignified. Also generosity, disinterestedness and self-sacrifice, when well dignified.

Malkuth of י (Cruelty, malice, revenge, injustice).

Therein rule רייאל and אומאל.

XXXVI
THE LORD OF HARMONIOUS CHANGE
Two of Disks or Pentacles

TWO wheels, disks or pentacles, similar to that of the Ace. They are united by a green-and-gold serpent, bound about them like a figure of 8. It holds its tail in its mouth. A White Radiant Angelic Hand holds the centre of the whole. No roses enter into this card. Above and below are the symbols of Jupiter and Capricorn. It is a revolving symbol.

The harmony of change, alternation of gain and loss; weakness and strength; ever-changing occupation; wandering, discontented with any fixed condition of things; now elated, then melancholy; industrious, yet unreliable; fortunate through prudence of management, yet sometimes unaccountably foolish; alternatively talkative and suspicious. Kind, yet wavering and inconsistent. Fortunate in journeying. Argumentative.

Chokmah of ה (Pleasant change, visit to friends).

Herein the Angels לכבאל and ושריה have rule.

XXXVII
THE LORD OF MATERIAL WORKS
Three of Pentacles

A WHITE-WINGED Angelic Hand, as before, holding a branch of a rose tree, of which two white rosebuds touch and surmount the topmost Pentacle. The Pentacles are arranged in an equilateral triangle. Above and below the symbols Mars and Capricorn.

Working and constructive force, building up, creation, erection; realization and increase of material things; gain in commercial transactions, rank; increase of substance, influence, cleverness in business, selfishness. Commencement of matters to be established later. Narrow and prejudiced. Keen in matters of gain; sometimes given to seeking after impossibilities.

Binah of ה (Business, paid employment, commercial transaction).

Herein are יחויה and להחיה Angelic Rulers.

XXXVIII
THE LORD OF EARTHLY POWER
Four of Pentacles

A HAND holding a branch of a rose tree, but without flowers or buds, save that in the centre is one fully blown white rose. Pentacles are disposed as on the points of a square; a rose in its centre. Symbols Sun and Capricorn above and below to represent the Decan.

Assured material gain: success, rank, dominion, earthy power, completed but leading to nothing beyond. Prejudicial, covetous, suspicious, careful and orderly, but discontented. Little enterprise or originality. According to dignity as usual.

Chesed of ה (Gain of money or influence: a present).

Herein do כוקיה and מנדאל bear rule.

XXXIX
THE LORD OF DEFEAT
Five of Swords

TWO Rayed Angelic Hands each holding two swords nearly upright, but falling apart of each other, right and left of the card. A third hand holds a sword upright in the centre as though it had disunited them. The petals of the rose, which in the four had been reinstated in the centre, are torn asunder and falling. Above and below are Venus and Aquarius for Decan.

Contest finished and decided against the person; failure, defeat, anxiety, trouble, poverty, avarice, grieving after gain, laborious, unresting; loss and vileness of nature; malicious, slanderous, lying, spiteful and tale-bearing. A busybody and separator of friends, hating to see peace and love between others. Cruel, yet cowardly, thankless and unreliable. Clever and quick in thought and speech. Feelings of pity easily roused, but unenduring.

Geburah of ן (Defeat, loss, malice, spite, slander, evil-speaking).

Herein the Angels אניאל and חעמיה bear rule.

XL
THE LORD OF EARNED SUCCESS
Six of Swords

TWO hands, as before, each holding two swords which cross in the centre. Rose re-established thereon. Mercury and Aquarius above and below, supported on the points of two short daggers or swords.

Success after anxiety and trouble; self-esteem, beauty, conceit, but sometimes modesty therewith; dominance, patience, labour, etc.

Tiphareth of ו (Labour, work, journey by water).

Ruled by the Great Angels רהעאל and ייהל.

XLI
THE LORD OF UNSTABLE EFFORT
Seven of Swords

TWO Angelic Radiating Hands as before, each holding three swords. A third hand holds up a single sword in the centre. The points of all the swords "just touch" each other, the central sword not altogether dividing them.

The Rose of the previous symbols of this suit is held up by the same hand which holds the central sword: as if the victory were at its disposal. Symbols of Moon and Aquarius.

Partial success. Yielding when victory is within grasp, as if the last reserves of strength were used up. Inclination to lose when on the point of gaining, through not continuing the effort. Love of abundance, fascinated by display, given to compliments, affronts and insolences, and to spy upon others. Inclined to betray confidences, not always intentionally. Rather vacillatory and unreliable.

Netzach of ו (Journey by land: in character untrustworthy).

Herein rule the Great Angels ההעאל and מיכאל.

XLII
THE LORD OF ABANDONED SUCCESS
Eight of Chalices

A WHITE Radiating Angelic Hand, holding a group of stems of lotuses or water-lilies. There are only two flowers shown, which bend over the two central cups, pouring into them a white water which fills them and runs over into the three lowest, which later are not yet filled. The three uppermost are quite empty. At the top and bottom of the card are symbols Saturn and Pisces.

Temporary success, but without further results. Thing thrown aside as soon as gained. Not lasting, even in the matter in hand. Indolence in success. Journeying from place to place. Misery and repining without cause. Seeking after riches. Instability.

Hod of ה (Success abandoned; decline of interest).

The Angels ruling are וליה and ילהיה.

XLIII
THE LORD OF MATERIAL HAPPINESS
Nine of Chalices

A WHITE Radiant Angelic Hand, issuing from a cloud holding lotus or water-lilies, one flower of which overhangs each cup; from it a white water pours. Cups are arranged in three rows of 3. Jupiter and Pisces above and below.

Complete and perfect realization of pleasure and happiness, almost perfect; self-praise, vanity, conceit, much talking of self, yet kind and lovable, and may be self-denying therewith. High-minded, not easily satisfied with small and limited ideas. Apt to be maligned through too much self-assumption. A good and generous, but sometimes foolish nature.

Yesod of ה (Complete success, pleasure and happiness, wishes fulfilled).

Therein rule the Angels סאליה and עריאל.

XLIV
THE LORD OF PERFECTED SUCCESS
Ten of Cups or Chalices

HAND, as usual, holding bunch of water-lilies or lotuses, whose flowers pour a white water into all the cups, which all run over. The uppermost cup is held sideways by a hand, and pours water into the left-hand upper cup. A single lotus flower surmounts the top cup, and is the source of the water that fills it. Above and below the symbols Mars and Pisces.

Permanent and lasting success and happiness, because inspired from above. Not so sensual as "Lord of Material Happiness," yet almost more truly happy. Pleasure, dissipation, debauchery, quietness, peacemaking. Kindness, pity, generosity, wantonness, waste, etc., according to dignity.

Malkuth of ה (Matter settled: complete good fortune).

Herein the Great Angels עשליה and מיהאל rule.

[This is not such a good card as stated. It represents boredom, and quarrelling arising therefrom; disgust springing from too great luxury. In particular it represents drug-habits, the sottish excess of pleasure and the revenge of nature.]

XLV

THE LORD OF DOMINION

Two of Wands

A WHITE Radiating Angelic hand, issuing from clouds, and grasping two crossed wands. Flames issue from the point of junction. On two small wands above and below, with flames of five issuing therefrom, are the symbols of Mars and Aries for the Decan.

Strength, domination, harmony of rule and of justice. Boldness, courage, fierceness, shamelessness, revenge, resolution, generous, proud, sensitive, ambitious, refined, restless, turbulent, sagacious withal, yet unforgiving and obstinate.

Chokmah of ' (Influence over others, authority, power, dominion).

Therein the Angels והואל and דניאל bear rule.

XLVI

THE LORD OF ESTABLISHED STRENGTH

Three of Wands

A WHITE Radiating Angelic Hand, as before, issuing from clouds and grasping three wands in the centre (two crossed, the third upright). Flames issue from the point of junction. Above and below are the symbols Sun and Aries.

Established force, strength, realization of hope. Completion of labour. Success after struggle. Pride, nobility, wealth, power, conceit. Rude self-assumption and insolence. Generosity, obstinacy, etc.

Binah of ׳ (Pride, arrogance, self-assertion).

Herein rule the Angels החשיה and עממיה.

[This card is much better than as described.]

XLVII
THE LORD OF PERFECTED WORK
Four of Wands

TWO White Radiating Angelic Hands, as before, issuing from clouds right and left of the card and clasped in the centre with the grip of the First Order, holding four wands or torches crossed. Flames issue from the point of junction. Above and below are two small flaming wands, with the symbols of Venus and Aries representing the Decan.

Perfection or completion of a thing built up with trouble and labour. Rest after labour, subtlety, cleverness, beauty, mirth, success in completion. Reasoning faculty, conclusions drawn from previous knowledge. Unreadiness, unreliable and unsteady through over-anxiety and hurriedness of action. Graceful in manner, at times insincere, etc.

Chesed of ׳ (Settlement, arrangement, completion).

Herein are ננאאל and ניתיאל Angelic rulers.

XLVIII
THE LORD OF MATERIAL TROUBLE
Five of Pentacles

A WHITE Radiant Angelic Hand issuing from clouds, and holding a branch of the white rose tree, but from which the roses are falling, and leaving no buds behind. Five Pentacles similar to the Ace. Above and below are Mercury and Taurus.

Loss of money or position. Trouble about material things. Labour, toil, land cultivation; building, knowledge and acuteness of earthly things, poverty, carefulness, kindness; sometimes money regained after severe toil and labour. Unimaginative, harsh, stern, determined, obstinate.

Geburah of ה (Loss of profession, loss of money, monetary anxiety).

Herein the angels מבהיה and פויאל rule.

XLIX
THE LORD OF MATERIAL SUCCESS
Six of Pentacles

A WHITE Radiant Angelic Hand holding a rose branch with white roses and buds, each of which touches a Pentacle. Pentacles are arranged in two columns of three each. Above and below are the symbols Taurus and Moon of the Decan.

Success and gain in material undertakings. Power, influence, rank, nobility, rule over the people. Fortunate, successful, liberal and just.

If ill dignified, may be purse-proud, insolent from excess, or prodigal.

Tiphareth of ה (Success in material things, prosperity in business).

Herein rule the Angels נממיה and ייליאל.

L
THE LORD OF SUCCESS UNFULFILLED

Seven of Pentacles

A WHITE Radiating Angelic Hand issuing from a cloud, and holding a white rose branch. Seven Pentacles arranged like the geomantic figure Rubeus. There are only five buds, which overhang, but do not touch the five uppermost Pentacles. Above and below are the Decan symbols, Saturn and Taurus respectively.

Promises of success unfulfilled. (Shewn, as it were, by the fact that the rosebuds do not come to anything.) Loss of apparently promising fortune. Hopes deceived and crushed. Disappointment, misery, slavery, necessity and baseness. A cultivator of land, and yet a loser thereby. Sometimes it denotes slight and isolated gains with no fruits resulting therefrom, and of no further account, though seeming to promise well.

Netzach of ה (Unprofitable speculations and employments; little gain for much labour).

Therein הרחאל and מצראל are ruling Angels.

LI
THE LORD OF SHORTENED FORCE
Eight of Swords

FOUR White Radiant Angelic Hands issuing from clouds, each holding two swords, points upwards; all the points touch near the top of the card. Hands issue, two at each bottom angle of the card. The pose of the other sword symbols is re-established in the centre. Above and below are the Decan symbols Jupiter and Gemini.

Too much force applied to small things: too much attention to detail at the expense of the principal and more important points. When ill dignified, these qualities produce malice, pettiness, and domineering characteristics. Patience in detail of study; great care in some things, counterbalanced by equal disorder in others. Impulsive; equally fond of giving or receiving money or presents; generous, clever, acute, selfish and without strong feeling of affection. Admires wisdom, yet applies it to small and unworthy objects.

Hod of ı (Narrow, restricted, petty, a prison).

Therein rule the Angels ומבאל and יההאל.

LII
THE LORD OF DESPAIR AND CRUELTY
Nine of Swords

FOUR Hands, as in the preceding figure, hold eight swords nearly upright, but with the points falling away from each other. A fifth hand holds a ninth sword upright in the centre, as if it had struck them asunder. No rose at all is shewn, as if it were not merely cut asunder, but utterly destroyed. Above and below are the Decan symbols Mars and Gemini.

Despair, cruelty, pitilessness, malice, suffering, want, loss, misery. Burden, oppression, labour, subtlety and craft, dishonesty, lying and slander.

Yet also obedience, faithfulness, patience, unselfishness, etc. According to dignity.

Yesod of ı (Illness, suffering, malice, cruelty, pain).

Therein do ענאל and מחיאל bear rule.

LIII

THE LORD OF RUIN
Ten of Swords

FOUR hands holding eight swords, as in the preceding symbol; the points falling away from each other. Two hands hold two swords crossed in the centre, as though their junction had disunited the others. No rose, flower or bud, is shewn. Above and below are Sun and Gemini, representing the Decan.

Almost a worse symbol than the Nine of Swords. Undisciplined, warring force, complete disruption and failure. Ruin of all plans and projects. Disdain, insolence and impertinence, yet mirth and jollity therewith. A marplot, loving to overthrow the happiness of others; a repeater of things; given to much unprofitable speech, and of many words. Yet clever, eloquent, etc., according to dignity.

Malkuth of ı (Ruin, death, defeat, disruption).

Herein the Angels דמביה and מנקאל reign.

LIV
THE LORD OF LOVE
Two of Chalices

A WHITE Radiant Hand, issuant from the lower part of the card from a cloud, holds lotuses. A lotus flower rises above water, which occupies the lower part of the card rising above the hand. From this flower rises a stem, terminating near the top of the card in another lotus, from which flows a sparkling white water, as from a fountain. Crossed on the stem just beneath are two dolphins, Argent and Or, on to which the water falls, and from which it pours in full streams, like jets of gold and silver, into two cups; which in their turn overflow, flooding the lower part of the card. Venus and Cancer above and below.

Harmony of masculine and feminine united. Harmony, pleasure, mirth, subtlety: but if ill dignified—folly, dissipation, waste, silly actions.

Chokmah of ה (Marriage, love, pleasure).

Therein rule the Angels אויאל and חבויה.

LV

THE LORD OF ABUNDANCE

Three of Chalices

A WHITE Radiating Hand, as before, holds a group of lotuses or water-lilies, from which two flowers rise on either side of, and overhanging the top cup; pouring into it the white water. Flowers in the same way pour white water into the lower cups. All the cups overflow; the topmost into the two others, and these upon the lower part of the card. Cups are arranged in an erect equilateral triangle. Mercury and Cancer above and below.

Abundance, plenty, success, pleasure, sensuality, passive success, good luck and fortune; love, gladness, kindness, liberality.

Binah of ה (Plenty, hospitality, eating and drinking, pleasure, dancing, new clothes, merriment).

Therein the Angels רהאל and יבמיה are lords.

LVI

THE LORD OF BLENDED PLEASURE

Four of Chalices

FOUR cups: the two upper overflowing into the two lower, which do not overflow. An Angelic Hand grasps a branch of lotus, from which ascends a stem bearing one flower at the top of the card, from which the white water flows into the two upper cups. From the centre two leaves pass right and left, making, as it were, a cross between the four cups. Above and below are the symbols Moon and Cancer for the Decan.

Success or pleasure approaching their end. A stationary period in happiness, which may, or may not, continue. It does not mean love and marriage so much as the previous symbol. It is too passive a symbol to represent perfectly complete happiness. Swiftness, hunting and pursuing. Acquisition by contention: injustice sometimes; some drawbacks to pleasure implied.

Chesed of ה (Receiving pleasure or kindness from others, but some discomfort therewith).

Therein rule the great Angels הייאל and מומיה.

OF THE THIRTY-SIX DECANS

HERE follow the descriptions of the smaller cards of the four suits, thirty-six in number, answering unto the thirty-six Decans of the Zodiac.

Commencing from the sign Aries, the "Central" Decans of each sign follow the order of the Days of the Week. Thus—

3 of Wands — Aries — Established Strength — Sun

6 of Pentacles — Taurus — Material Success — Moon

9 of Swords — Gemini — Despair and Cruelty — Mars

3 of Cups — Cancer — Abundance — Mercury

6 of Wands — Leo — Victory — Jupiter

9 of Pentacles — Virgo — Material Gain — Venus

3 of Swords — Libra — Sorrow — Saturn

6 of Cups — Scorpio — Pleasure — Sun

9 of Wands — Sagittarius — Great Strength — Moon

3 of Pentacles — Capricorn — Material Works — Mars

6 of Swords — Aquarius — Earned Success — Mercury

9 of Cups — Pisces — Material Happiness — Jupiter

Being thus the Four Threes, Sixes, and Nines.

The first and third Decans follow the same order: Sunday beginning the First Decan of Virgo and in the Third Decans of Gemini and Capricorn.

There being thirty-six Decans and seven Planets, it follows that one of the latter must rule over one more Decan than the others. This is the Planet Mars, to which are allotted the last Decan of Pisces, and the first of Aries, because the long cold of the winter requires a great energy to overcome it, and initiate spring.

And the beginning of the Decanates is from the royal Star of Leo, the great Star Cor Leonis: and therefore is the first Decan that of Saturn in Leo.

MEANINGS OF THE SEPHIROTH IN RELATION TO THE SMALL CARDS

Here follow the general meanings of the small cards of the suits, as classified under the nine Sephiroth below Kether.

חכמה — The Four Twos symbolize the Powers of the King and Queen just uniting and initiating the Force; but before the Prince and Princess are thoroughly brought into action. Therefore do they generally imply the initiation and fecundation of a thing.

בינה — Realization of action owing to the Prince being produced. The central symbol on each card. Action definitely commenced for good or evil.

חסד — Perfection, realization, completion: making a matter settled and fixed.

גבורה — Opposition, strife and struggle: war; obstacle to the thing in hand. Ultimate success or failure is otherwise shewn.

תפארת — Definite accomplishment. Thing carried out.

נצח — Generally shew a force transcending the Material Plane: and is like unto a Crown; which, indeed, is powerful, but requireth one capable of wearing it. The Sevens then shew a possible result: which is dependent on the action then taken. They depend much on the symbols that accompany them.

הוד — Solitary success: i.e. success in the matter for the time being: but not leading to much result apart from the thing itself.

יסוד — Very great fundamental force. Executive power, because they restore a firm basis. Powerful for good or evil.

מלכות — Fixed, culminated, complete Force, whether good or evil. The matter thoroughly and definitely determined. Ultimating Force.

BRIEF MEANING OF TWENTY-TWO KEYS

0. IF the question refers to spiritual matters, the Fool means idea, thought, spirituality, that which endeavours to transcend Earth. But if question is material, it means folly, stupidity, eccentricity, or even mania.

1. Skill, wisdom, adaptation, craft, cunning, or occult wisdom or power.

2. Change, alternation, increase and decrease, fluctuation; whether for good or evil depends on the dignity.

3. Beauty, happiness, pleasure, success. But with very bad dignity it means luxury, dissipation.

4. War, conquest, victory, strife, ambition.

5. Divine wisdom, manifestation, explanation, teaching, occult force voluntarily invoked.

6. Inspiration (passive, mediumistic), motive power, action.

7. Triumph, victory, health (sometimes unstable).

8. Eternal justice. Strength and force, but arrested as in act of judgment. May mean law, trial, etc.

9. Wisdom from on high. Active divine inspiration. Sometimes "unexpected current."

10. Good fortune, happiness (within bounds). Intoxication of success.

11. Courage, strength, fortitude, power passing on to action. Obstinacy.

12. Enforced sacrifice, punishment, loss, fatal and not voluntary, suffering.

13. Time, age, transformation, change involuntary (as opposed to 18, Pisces). Or death, destruction (only latter with special cards). [Specially, a sudden and quite unexpected change.]

14. Combination of forces, realization, action (material effect, good or evil).

15. Materiality, material force, material temptation, obsession.

16. Ambition, fighting, war, courage, or destruction, danger, fall, ruin.

17. Hope, faith, unexpected help. Or dreaminess, deceived hope, etc.

18. Dissatisfaction, voluntary change. Error, lying, falsity, deception. This card is very sensitive to dignity.

19. Glory, gain, riches. With very evil cards it means arrogance, display, vanity.

20. Final decision, judgment, sentence, determination of a matter without appeal, on its plane.

21. The matter itself. Synthesis, world, kingdom. Usually denotes actual subject of question, and therefore depends entirely on accompanying cards.

[This table is very unsatisfactory. Each card must be most carefully meditated, taking all its correspondences, and a clear idea formed.]

Princes and Queens shew almost always actual men and women connected with the matter.

But the Kings (Knights) sometime represent coming or going of a matter, according as they face.

The Princesses shew opinions, thoughts, ideas, either in harmony with or opposed to, the subject.

A Majority of Wands — Energy, opposition, quarrel.

A Majority of Cups — Pleasure, merriment.

A Majority of Swords — Trouble, sadness, sickness, death.

A Majority of Pentacles — Business, money, possessions.

A Majority of Keys — Strong forces beyond the Querent's control.

A Majority of Court Cards — Society, meetings of many persons.

A Majority of Aces — Strength generally. Aces are always strong cards.

4 Aces — Great power and force.

3 Aces — Riches, success.

4 Kings (Knights) — Swiftness, rapidity.

3 Kings (Knights) — Unexpected meetings. Knights, in general, shew news.

4 Queens — Authority, influence.

3 Queens — Powerful friends.

4 Princes — Meetings with the great.

3 Princes — Rank and honour.

4 Princesses — New ideas or plans.

3 Princesses — Society of the young.

4 Tens — Anxiety, responsibility.

3 Tens — Buying and selling (commerce).

4 Nines — Added responsibilities.

3 Nines — Much correspondence.

4 Eights — Much news.

3 Eights — Much journeying.

4 Sevens — Disappointments.

3 Sevens — Treaties and compacts.

4 Sixes — Pleasure.

3 Sixes — Gain, success.

4 Fives — Order, regularity.

3 Fives — Quarrels, fights.

4 Fours — Rest, peace.

3 Fours — Industry.

4 Threes — Resolution, determination.

3 Threes — Deceit.

4 Twos — Conferences, conversations.

3 Twos — Reorganization, recommendation.

OF THE DIGNITIES

A CARD is strong or weak, well dignified or ill dignified, according to the cards next to it on either side.

Cards of the same suit on either side strengthen it greatly, for good or evil according to their nature.

Cards of opposite natures on either side weaken it greatly, for either good or evil.

Swords are inimical to Pentacles.

Wands are inimical to Cups.

Swords are friendly with Cups and Wands.

Wands are friendly with Swords and Pentacles.

If a card fall between two others which are mutually contrary, it is not much affected by either.

A METHOD OF DIVINATION BY THE TAROT

[This method is that given to students of the grade Adept Adeptus Minor in the R. R. et A. C. But it has been revised and improved, while certain safeguards have been introduced in order to make its abuse impossible.—O.M.]

1.—THE Significator.

Choose a card to represent the Querent, using your knowledge or judgment of his character rather than dwelling on his physical characteristics.

2.—Take the cards in your left hand. In the right hand hold the wand over them, and say: I invoke thee, I A O, that thou wilt send H R U, the great Angel that is set over the operations of this Secret Wisdom, to lay his hand invisibly upon these consecrated cards of art, that thereby we may obtain true knowledge of hidden things, to the glory of thine ineffable Name. Amen.

3.—Hand the cards to Querent, and bid him think of the question attentively, and cut.

4.—Take the cards as cut, and hold as for dealing.

First Operation

This shows the situation of the Querent at the time when he consults you.

1. The pack being in front of you, cut, and place the top half to the left.

2. Cut each pack again to the left.

3. These four stacks represent I H V H, from right to left.

4. Find the Significator. If it be in the Yod pack, the question refers to work, business, etc.; if in the He pack, to love, marriage, or pleasure; if in the Vau pack, to trouble, loss, scandal, quarrelling, etc; if in the He final pack, to money, goods, and such purely material matters.

5. Tell the Querent what he has come for: if wrong, abandon the divination.

6. If right, spread out the pack containing the Significator, face upwards.

Count the cards from him, in the direction in which he faces.

The counting should include the card from which you count.

For Knights, Queens and Princes, count 4.

For Princesses, count 7.

For Aces, count 11.

For small cards, count according to the number.

For trumps, count 3 for the elemental trumps; 9 for the planetary trumps; 12 for the Zodiacal trumps.

Make a "story" of these cards. This story is that of the beginning of the affair.

7. Pair the cards on either side of the Significator, then those outside them, and so on. Make another "story," which should fill in the details omitted in the first.

8. If this story is not quite accurate, do not be discouraged. Perhaps the Querent himself does not know everything. But the main lines ought to be laid

down firmly, with correctness, or the divination should be abandoned.

Second Operation

Development of the Question

1.—Shuffle, and let Querent cut as before.

2.—Deal cards into twelve stacks, for the twelve astrological houses of heaven.

3.—Find the Significator: this will shew in what part of his affairs the question lies.

4.—Count and pair as before.

Third Operation

Further Development

1.—Shuffle, etc., as before.

2.—Deal cards into twelve stacks for the twelve signs.

3.—Find Significator.

4.—Count and pair as before.

Fourth Operation

Penultimate   Aspects

1.—Shuffle, etc., as before.

2.—Find the Significator: deal the cards into ten packs in the form of the Tree of Life.

3.—Count and pair as before.

[Note that the nature of each Decan is shewn by the small card attributed to it, and by the symbols given in Liber DCCLXXVII, cols. 149-151.]

Fifth Operation

Final Result

1.—Shuffle, etc., as before.

2.—Deal into ten packs in the form of the Tree of Life.

3.—Make up your mind where the Significator should be, as before; but failure does not here necessarily imply that the divination has gone astray.

4.—Count and pair as before.

[Note that one cannot tell at what part of the divination the present time occurs. Usually Op. 1 seems to indicate the past history of the question; but not always so. Experience will teach. Sometimes a new current of high help may show the moment of consultation.

I may add that in material matters this method is extremely valuable. I have been able to work out the most complex problems in minute detail. O. M.]

LIBER

GAIAS

SVB FIGVRÂ

XCVI

A HANDBOOK
OF GEOMANCY

V

A∴A∴

Publication in Class B

"Direct not thy mind to the vast surfaces of the earth; for the Plant of Truth grows not upon the ground. Nor measure the motions of the Sun, collecting rules, for he is carried by the Eternal Will of the Father, and not for your sake alone. Dismiss from your mind the impetuous course of the Moon, for she moveth always by the power of Necessity. The progression of the Stars was not generated for your sake. The wide aerial flight of birds gives no true knowledge, nor the dissection of the entrails of victims; these are all mere toys, the basis of mercenary fraud: flee from these if you would enter the sacred paradise of piety where Virtue, Wisdom, and Equity are assembled."

ZOROASTER.

```
M A C A N E H
A R O L U S E
D I R U C U N
A L U H U L A
S E R U R O C
U N E L I R A
L U S A D A M
```

CHAPTER I

ATIRIBUTIONS OF GEOMANTIC FIGURES TO PLANETS, ZODIAC, AND RULING GENII

-	SIGN	EL.	GEOM. FIG.	SEX	NAME AND MEANING	GENIUS	RULER	PLANET
1	c·p	,0,.	• • •	M.	Puer Boy, yellow, beardless	Malchidael	Bartzabel	6
2	◆	9	∴	F.	Amissio Loss, comprehended without	Asmodel	Kedemel	9
3	II	8	∷	M.	Albus White, fair	Ambriel	Taphthartha-ralh	◆
4	§	"v	•••.	F.	Populus People, congregation	Muriel	Chasmodai	J)
5	Ji	,0,.	∵	M.	Fortuna Major Greater fortune, greater aid, safeguard entering	Verchiel	Sorath	0
6	fQl	9	∴	F.	Conjunctio Conjunction, assembling	Hamaliel	Taphthartha-rath	◆
7	£1	8	∴	M.	Puella A girl, beautiful	Zuriel	Kedemel	9
8	m.	"v	⸭	F.	Rubeus Red, reddish	Barchiel	Bartzabel	6
9	?	,0,.	∴	M.	Acquisit:io Obtaining, comprehending without	Advachiel	Hismael	1/
10	YJ	9	• •	F.	Career A prison, bound	Hanael	Zazel	9
11	⸬	8	⁖	M.	Tristitia Sadness, damned, cross	Cambiel	Zazel	9
12	l·t	"v	⁞	F.	Lretltia Joy, laughing, healthy, bearded	Anmixiel	Hismael	1/
13	t'5	,0,.	• •	F.	Cauda Draconis The threshold lower, or going out	Zazel and Bartzabel	Zazel and Bartzabel	ij d
14	Q	9	• •	M	Caput Draconis The Head, the threshold entering, the upper threshold	Hjsmael and Kedmel	Hismael and Kedmel	4 9
15	Ji	8	• •	M.	Fortuna Minor Lesser Fortune, lesser aid, safe-guard going out.	Verchiel	Sorath	0
16	§	"v	• •	F.	Via Way journey	Muriel	Chasmodai	J)

CHAPTER II

THE MODE OF DIVINING-MOTHERS-DAUGHTERS- NEPHEWS-WITNESSES-JUDGE-RECONCILER-PART OF FORTUNE

TIDNK fixedly of the demand; with a pencil mark 16 lines of points or dashes. Find whether number of points in each line is odd or even. For odd •; for even • •. Lines 1-4 give the first mother; lines 5-8 the second; and so on.

EXAMPLE

4		3		2		1	
• •	10	• •	12	•	15	•	15
•	1	• •	6	• •	16	•	1
•	1		9	•	15	•	16
• •	10	•	7	• •	14	• •	1

[The small Arabic numbers refer to the chance number of dashes.]

Use clean (virgin) paper; place appropriate Pentagram (either with or without a circumscribed circle) invoking. If a circle, draw this first. Sigil of Ruler to which nature of question most refers should be placed in the Pentagram thus:

1:> Agriculture, sorrow, death.

◆ Good fortune, feasting, church preferment.

d War, victory, fighting.

0 Power, magistracy.

9 Love, music, pleasure.

◆ Science, learning, knavery.

J) Travelling, fishing, &c.

In diagram, p. 6, the Sigil of Hismael should be used.

In marking points fix attention on Sigil and on the question proposed; the hand should not be moved from the paper till complete. It is convenient to rule lines, to guide the eye.

The daughters are derived by reading the mothers horizontally.

The four nephews, Figures IX-XII, are thus formed: IX = I + II read vertically, added and taken as odd or even. So also XIII = IX + X, and XV = XIII + XIV.

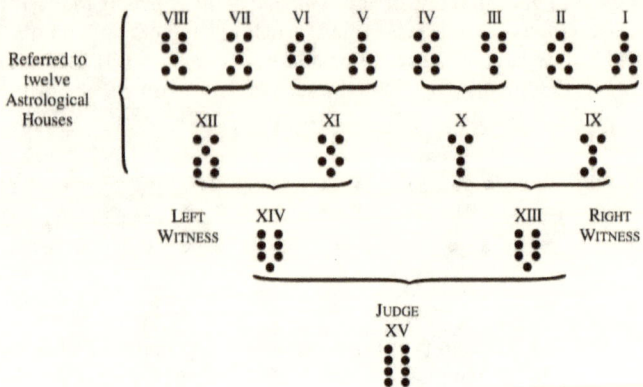

These last three are merely aids to general judgement. If the judge be good the figure is good, and *vice-versâ*.

The Reconciler = I + XV.

To find the Part of Fortune ⊕ (ready money or cash belonging to the Querent), add points of the figures I-XII, divide by 12, and remainder shows figure. Here I + II + . . . + XII = 74 points = 6 ×12 + 2. ∴ ⊕ falls with ∴∴ (II).

CHAPTER III

THE meaning of the twelve Houses is to be found, primarily, in any text-book of Astrology. Knowledge is to be enlarged and corrected by constant study and practice.

Place the figures thus:

I	10th	IV	1h	VII	5th	X	3rd
II	Ase.	V	11th	VIII	8th	XI	6th
III	4th	VI	2nd	IX	12th	XII	9th

EXAMPLE

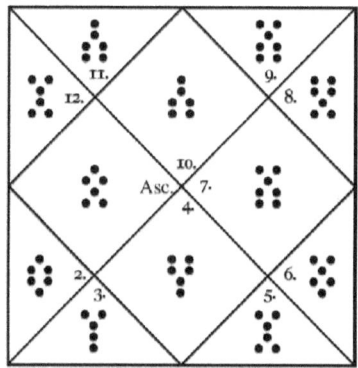

119

CHAPTER IV

TABLES OF WITNESSES AND JUDGE

THE tables are classed by the Left Witness.

The judgement concerning a wife (*e.g.*) will hold good for all demands of the 7th House.

So of the others.

L.W. POPULUS		R.W. J.	R.W. J.	R.W. J.	R.W. J.	R.W. J.	R.W. J.	R.W. J.	R.W. J.
Life, &c.	1	Mod.	Good	Good	Mod.	Mod.	Evil	Good	Mod.
Money, &c.	2	Mod.	Good	Good	Bad	Mod.	Evil	Mod.	Good
Rank, &c.	3	Mod.	Good	Good	Mod.	Good	Mod.	Mod.	Bad
Property	4	Mod.	Good	Good	Bad	Good	Bad	Mod.	Good
Wife, &c,	5	Good	Good	Bad	Good	Good	Bad	Good	Bad
Sex of Child	6	5*	Evil	Dau.	Son	Dau.	Dau.	5	Dau.
Sickness	7	Asc.	Health	Soon health	Health	Perilous	Health	Health	Asc.
Prison	8	Come out	Out	Soon out	Out for nothing	Long	Out	Die there	Die there
Journey	9	Good by water	Slow	Medium	Good by water	Evil	Medium	Medium	Evil
Thing Lost	10	Found	Found	Part found	Not found	Found	Lost	Found	Part found

* Arabic numbers mean that the judgement is determined by the figure in that House of Heaven.

LIBER GAIAS

L.W. LÆTITIA		R.W. J.	R.W. J.	R.W. J.	R.W. J.	R.W. J.	R.W. J.	R.W. J.	R.W. J.
Life, &c.	1	Good and long	Med.	Med.	Evil	Med.	Med.	Med.	Good
Money, &c.	2	Increase	Evil	Med.	Med.	Good	Evil	Med.	Med.
Rank, &c.	3	Good dignity	Med.	Med.	Good	Good	Evil	Med.	Med.
Property	4	Good	Med.	Med.	Good	Good	Evil	Med.	Evil
Wife, &c,	5	Good	Med.	Med.	Evil	Good	Evil	Med.	Good
Sex of Child	6	Son	Dau.	Dau.	Dau.	5	Son	5	Son
Sickness	7	Health	11	Asc	Danger-ous	Health	Health	Health	5
Prison	8	Late out	Come out	Come out	Come out	Soon out	Run away	Escape and re-capture	Come out
Journey	9	Good in end	Hurtful	Evil	Evil	Good	Evil	Return	Good by water
Thing Lost	10	Found	Found	Part found	Part found	Part found	Part yielded	Part found	Part found

L.W. VIA		R.W. J.	R.W. J.	R.W. J.	R.W. J.	R.W. J.	R.W. J.	R.W. J.	R.W. J.
Life, &c.	1	Med.	Evil	Med.	Med.	Med.	Evil	Med.	Med.
Money, &c.	2	Evil	Evil	Med.	Med.	Med.	Med.	Med.	Med.
Rank, &c.	3	Med.	Good	Med.	Med.	Evil	Evil	Med.	Med.
Property	4	Evil	Good	Med.	Med.	Med.	Good	Med.	Med.
Wife, &c,	5	Good	Good	Med.	Evil	Evil	Evil	Med.	Med.
Sex of Child	6	Son	Dau.	5	5	5	5	Son	5
Sickness	7	Health	Danger-ous	Health	Death	Death	Death	Health	Health
Prison	8	Out for nothing	Evil	Come out	Not out	Not out	Not out	Come out	Soon out
Journey	9	Good by water	Good by water	Slack	Return	Return	Late	Late	Good
Thing Lost	10	Not found	Not found	Part yielded	Found	Found	Part found	Little found	Not found

L.W. FORTUNA MAJOR	R.W. J.	R.W. J.	R.W. J.	R.W. J.	R.W. J.	R.W. J.	R.W. J.	R.W. J.
Life, &c. 1	Good	Evil	Good	Med.	Med.	Med.	Good	Med.
Money, &c. 2	Good	Evil	Good	Med.	Med.	Med.	Good	Med.
Rank, &c. 3	Possibility good	Evil	Good	Good	Good	Med.	Good	Good
Property 4	Good	Evil	Good	Med.	Med.	Med.	Good	Evil
Wife, &c, 5	Good	Evil	Good	Good	Good	Evil	Good	Evil
Sex of Child 6	5	Son	Son	5	Son	Dau.	5	5
Sickness 7	Health	Health	Good	Asc.	Health	Perilous	Health	Health
Prison 8	Come out	Late	Come out	Die there	Come out	With harm	Come out	Soon out
Journey 9	Good with speed	Evil	Difficult	Med.	Soon return	Late	Good	Very good
Thing Lost 10	Found	Not found	Found	Found	Part found	Not found	Found	Not found

L.W. ALBUS	R.W. J.	R.W. J.	R.W. J.	R.W. J.	R.W. J.	R.W. J.	R.W. J.	R.W. J.
Life, &c. 1	Evil	Good	Evil	Suffic'nt	Evil	Good	Evil	Med.
Money, &c. 2	Evil	Good	Med.	Good	Med.	Good	Evil	Med.
Rank, &c. 3	Evil	Good	Evil	Good	Evil	Good	Evil	Med.
Property 4	Evil	Good	Evil	Good	Med.	Good	Evil	Med.
Wife, &c, 5	Evil	Evil	Med.	Good	Evil	Good	Evil	Med.
Sex of Child 6	Dau. die	5	Dau.	5	Dau.	5	Dau.	Dau.
Sickness 7	Death	Health	Death	Health	Death	Health	Health	Asc.
Prison 8	Perilous	Late	Not out	Come out	Die there	Run away	Come out	Come out
Journey 9	Med.	Good	Evil	Good	Difficult	Slow	Med.	V. good by water
Thing Lost 10	Not found	Not found	Not found	Part found	Part found	Found	Not found	Part found

LIBER GAIAS

L.W. RUBEUS	R.W. J.	R.W. J.	R.W. J.	R.W. J.	R.W. J.	R.W. J.	R.W. J.	R.W. J.
Life, &c. 1	Good	Med.	Med.	Good	Evil	Med.	Evil	Very evil
Money, &c. 2	Good	Med.	Med.	Good	Evil	Good	Evil	Very evil
Rank, &c. 3	Good	Med.	Med.	Med.	Evil	Good	Evil	Very evil
Property 4	Good	Med.	Med.	Good	Evil	Med.	Evil	Very evil
Wife, &c, 5	Very good	Evil	Good	Med.	Evil	Good	Evil	Immoral
Sex of Child 6	Son	Dau.	Dau.	Son.	Dau.	5	5	5
Sickness 7	Health	Health	Death	Health	Health	Long sick	In danger	Perilous
Prison 8	Come out	Difficult	Evil	Evil	Come out	Soon out	Doubtful	Death
Journey 9	Difficult	Evil	Evil	Evil	Evil	Slow	Evil	Robbed
Thing Lost 10	Part found	Part yielded	Not found	Found	Not found	Found	Not found	Not found

L.W. TRISTITIA	R.W. J.	R.W. J.	R.W. J.	R.W. J.	R.W. J.	R.W. J.	R.W. J.	R.W. J.
Life, &c. 1	Evil	Suffic'nt	Evil	Med.	Evil	Med.	Good	Evil
Money, &c. 2	Med.	Suffic'nt	Evil	Med.	Evil	Med.	Good	Very evil
Rank, &c. 3	Evil	Suffic'nt	Evil	Evil	Evil	Good	Good	Evil
Property 4	Good	Suffic'nt	Evil	Evil	Evil	Evil	Good	Very evil
Wife, &c, 5	Evil	Suffic'nt	Evil	Evil	Evil	Evil	Good	Evil
Sex of Child 6	5	Dau.	Son	Dau.	5	5	Dau.	5
Sickness 7	Death	Death	Evil	Evil	Evil	Health	Health	Perilous
Prison 8	Death	Death	Evil	Evil	Evil	Come out	Long	Hard
Journey 9	Evil	Evil	Evil	Evil	Evil	Very late	Late	Med.
Thing Lost 10	Not found	Found	Not found	Not found	Not found	Not found	Found	Not found

L.W. PUELLA		R.W. J.	R.W. J.	R.W. J.	R.W. J.	R.W. J.	R.W. J.	R.W. J.	R.W. J.
Life, &c.	1	Med.	Med.	Good	Good	Evil	Med.	Good	Evil
Money, &c.	2	Med.	Good	Good	Good	Med.	Med.	Good	Evil
Rank, &c.	3	Evil	Good	V. good	Good	Evil	Good	Good	Evil
Property	4	Evil	Good	Med	Good	Med.	Med.	Good	Evil
Wife, &c.	5	Med.	Good	Good	Good	Evil	Med.	Good	Med.
Sex of Child	6	Dau.	Son	5	5	5	5	Dau.	5
Sickness	7	Asc.	Health	Dangerous	Asc.	Health	Health	Long	Health
Prison	8	Out by ill means	Come out	Come out	Good end	Come out	Come out	Long	Come out
Journey	9	Perilous	Good	Good by ▽	Good	Perilous	Slow	Good	Med.
Thing Lost	10	Part found	Found	Part found	Found	Not found	Not found	Found	Part found

L.W. PUER		R.W. J.	R.W. J.	R.W. J.	R.W. J.	R.W. J.	R.W. J.	R.W. J.	R.W. J.
Life, &c.	1	Good	Evil	Evil	Evil	Med.	Evil	Med.	Evil
Money, &c.	2	Good	Somewhat good	Evil	Evil	Med.	Evil	Med.	Evil
Rank, &c.	3	Good	Med.	Evil	Evil	Med.	Evil	Med.	Evil
Property	4	Med.	Med.	Evil	Evil	Med.	Evil	Med.	Evil
Wife, &c.	5	Good	Med.	Evil	Evil	Med.	Evil	Med.	Evil
Sex of Child	6	Son	Dau.	5	Dau.	Son	Dau.	Son.	Dau.
Sickness	7	Health	Soon die	Asc.	Death	Health	Perilous	Health	Evil
Prison	8	Well out	Soon out	Dangerous	Die there	Come out	Perilous	Come out	Evil
Journey	9	Return	Med.	Spoiled	Evil	Med.	Evil	Med.	Evil
Thing Lost	10	Found	Part found	Not found	Not found	Found	Not found	Found	Not found

LIBER GAIAS

L.W. CAPUT DRACONIS		R.W. J.	R.W. J.	R.W. J.	R.W. J.	R.W. J.	R.W. J.	R.W. J.	R.W. J.
Life, &c.	1	Evil	Good	V. good	Evil	Evil	Good	Evil	Good
Money, &c.	2	Evil	Good	V. good	Suffic'nt	Med.	V. good	Evil	V. good
Rank, &c.	3	Evil	Good	V. good	Evil	Good	Good	Evil	Good
Property	4	Evil	Good	V. good	Med.	Suffic'nt	Good	Evil	Good
Wife, &c,	5	Evil	Med.	Good	Evil	Med.	Med.	Evil	Good
Sex of Child	6	Dau.	5	5	Dau.	Son	Son	Dau.	Son
Sickness	7	Asc.	Health	Asc.	Health	Good end	Health	Health	Health
Prison	8	Long	Perilous	Come out	Hard	6	Soon out	Come out	Out late
Journey	9	Evil	Med.	Good by ▽	Evil	Evil	Good	Evil	V. good
Thing Lost	10	Not found	Found	Found	Found	Part found	Found	Not found	Found

L.W. CAUDA DRACONIS		R.W. J.	R.W. J.	R.W. J.	R.W. J.	R.W. J.	R.W. J.	R.W. J.	R.W. J.
Life, &c.	1	Med.	Evil	Very evil	Tolerable	Evil	Med.	Good	Evil
Money, &c.	2	Good	Evil	Very evil	Good	Med.	Suffic'nt	Good	Evil
Rank, &c.	3	Med.	Evil	Very evil	Med.	Evil	Suffic'nt	Good	Evil
Property	4	Good	Evil	Very evil	Med.	Evil	Suffic'nt	Good	Med.
Wife, &c,	5	Med.	Evil	Very evil	Med.	Evil	Evil	Med.	Very evil
Sex of Child	6	Son	5	5	5	5	5	Son and live	5
Sickness	7	Health	Perilous	Death	Death	Death	Perilous	Health	Asc.
Prison	8	Good end	Out with pain	Death	Come out	Come out punished	Come out	Soon out	Dangerous
Journey	9	Evil	Evil	Very evil	Med.	Evil	Evil	Good	Very evil
Thing Lost	10	Found	Not found	Not found	Found	Not found	Part found	Found	Not found

L.W. ACQUISITIO		R.W. J.	R.W. J.	R.W. J.	R.W. J.	R.W. J.	R.W. J.	R.W. J.	R.W. J.
Life, &c.	1	Good	Evil	V. good	Med.	Good	Med.	Med.	Good
Money, &c.	2	Med.	Evil	V. good	Evil	Good	Med.	Med.	Good
Rank, &c.	3	Med.	Med.	V. good	Evil	Good	Med.	Med.	Good
Property	4	Med.	Evil	V. good	Evil	Good	Med.	Med.	Good
Wife, &c,	5	Good	Evil	Good	Evil	Good	Med.	Med.	Good
Sex of Child	6	5	Son	5	5	Son	Dau.	5	Son
Sickness	7	Health	Health	Health	Health	Health	Health	Asc.	In danger
Prison	8	Death	Come out	Come out	Come out	Long	Come out	Late out	Slow
Journey	9	Med.	Good	Good	Med.	Soon return	Med.	Evil	Slow
Thing Lost	10	Found	Not found	Found	Not found	Found	Found	Found	Found

L.W. AMISSIO		R.W. J.	R.W. J.	R.W. J.	R.W. J.	R.W. J.	R.W. J.	R.W. J.	R.W. J.
Life, &c.	1	Good	Med.	Evil	Med.	Med.	Med.	Evil	Evil
Money, &c.	2	Good	Med.	Evil	Med.	Med.	Evil	Evil	Med.
Rank, &c.	3	Med.	Med.	Evil	Good	Med.	Med.	Evil	Evil
Property	4	Med.	Med.	Evil	Med.	Med.	Evil	Evil	Med.
Wife, &c,	5	Med.	Med.	Evil	Med.	Med.	Evil	Evil	Evil
Sex of Child	6	5	Son	5	5	Dau.	Son	5	5
Sickness	7	The end health	Health	Perilous	Health	Health	Health	Death	Health
Prison	8	Long	Good end	Hard	Soon out	Come out	Come out	Out in the end	Die there
Journey	9	Good	Med.	Evil	Good	Med.	Med.	Evil	Not begun
Thing Lost	10	Not found	Found	Not found	Not found	Not found	Not found	Part found	Not found

LIBER GAIAS

L.W. CONJUNCTIO		R.W. J.	R.W. J.	R.W. J.	R.W. J.	R.W. J.	R.W. J.	R.W. J.	R.W. J.
Life, &c.	1	Good	Med.	Med.	Good	Evil	Good	Med.	Med.
Money, &c.	2	Good	Med.	Med.	Good	Evil	Good	Med.	Med.
Rank, &c.	3	Good	Med.	Med.	V. good	Evil	Good	Med.	Hard
Property	4	Good	Med.	Med.	V. good	Evil	Good	Med.	Med.
Wife, &c,	5	Good	Evil	Med.	V. good	Evil	Good	Good	Med.
Sex of Child	6	Son	5	5	Dau.	5	Son	Dau.	Dau.
Sickness	7	Long & pining	Death	Death	Asc.	Asc.	Health	Perilous	Hard
Prison	8	Long time	Out with fear	Perilous	Long	Good	Come out	Come out	Long
Journey	9	Slow	Med.	Good by ▽	Good	Med.	Evil	Slow	Hard
Thing Lost	10	Found	Found	Not found	Found	Not found	Found	Not found	Found

L.W. CARCER		R.W. J.	R.W. J.	R.W. J.	R.W. J.	R.W. J.	R.W. J.	R.W. J.	R.W. J.
Life, &c.	1	Good	Med.	Good	Good	Med.	Suffic'nt	Evil	Med.
Money, &c.	2	Good	Evil	Good	Med.	Med.	Suffic'nt	Evil	Med.
Rank, &c.	3	Evil	Med.	Good	Good	Med.	Med.	Evil	Med.
Property	4	Med.	Evil	Good	Good	Med.	Suffic'nt	Med.	Good
Wife, &c,	5	Evil	Med.	Good	Good	Med.	Suffic'nt	Evil	Good
Sex of Child	6	Dau.	5	Son	Dau.	5	5	5	Dau.
Sickness	7	Health	Health	Health	Health	Health	Health	Perilous	Dangerous
Prison	8	Good end	Soon out	Late out	Come out	Come out	Come out	Evil	Late out
Journey	9	Slow	Good	Slow	Slow	Slow	Slow	Difficult	Evil
Thing Lost	10	Found	Little found	Part found	Part found	Part found	Not found	Not found	Be found

L.W. FORTUNA MINOR		R.W. J	R . W.J	R .W. J	R.W...J	R.W....J	R.W...J	R . W.J	R .W J
Life, &c.	1	Good	Med.	Med.	Good	Evil	Med.	Good	Med.
Money, &c.	2	Good	Med.	Med.	Good	Evil	Evil	Good	Med.
Rank, &c.	3	Good	Med.	Med.	Good	Evil	Med.	Good	Evil
Property	4	Good	Med.	Med.	Good	Evil	Med.	Evil	Med.
Wife, &c,	5	Good	Med.	Med.	Good	Evil	Med.	Evil	Med.
Sex of Child	6	5	5	S	Son	Dau.	Son	Dau.	Dau.
Sickness	7	Health	Death	Health	Health	Ase.	Health	Health quickly	Perilous
Prison	8	Come out	Come out	Hard prison	Longin prison	Come out	Sorrow	Come out	Die
Journey	9	Good	Med.	Good	Late good	Good	Med.	Med.	Evil
Thing Lost	10	Found	Found	Part found	Found	N0t found	Not found	Not found	Found

CHAPTER V

THE GENERAL MEANING OF THE SIXTEEN FIGURES IN THE TWELVE HOUSES

HEREIN follows a set of general tables of the sixteen figures in the twelve Houses, for the better convenience of forming a general judgement of the scheme. Under the head of each figure separately is given its general effect in whatever House it may happen to fall.

Thus, by taking the House signifying the thing demanded, and also that signifying the end of the matter (fourth House), and noticing what figures fall therein, you may find by these tables their general effect in that position.

LIBERGAIAS

ACQUISITIO		FORTUNA MrNOR	
	1	Happy success in all things	
	2	Very prosperous	
	3	Favour and riches	
	4	Good fortune and success	
	S	Good success	
	6	Good, esp. agreeing with 5'h	
	7	Reasonably good	
	8	Rather good, not very. the sick die	
	9	Good in all	
	10	Good in suits. very prosperous	
	11	Good in all	
	12	Evil, pain, and loss	

		FORTUNA MrNOR
Good in any matter where a person wishes to proceed quickly.	1	Speed in victory or love; but choleric
	2	Very good
	3	Good but wrathful
	4	Haste; rather evil. exc. for peace
	S	Good in all
	6	Medium in all
	7	Evil, exc. for war or love
	8	Evil generally
	9	Good, but choleric
	10	Good. exc for peace
	n	Good. esp. for love
	12	Good, exc. for alteration or serving another

AMrSSIO		LETITIA	
Gd.for loss of substance, and some-times for love, but v. bad for gain.		Ill in all but for prisoners	
		V. evil for money. good for love	
	3	Ul end, exc. in quarrels	
	4	Ill in all	
	S	Evil, exc. for agriculture	
	6	Rather evil, exc. for love	
	7	V. good for love, otherwise evil	
	8	Excellent in all questions	
	9	Evil in all	
	10	Evil, exc. for women's favour	
	11	Good for love, otherwise bad	
	12	Evil in all	

		LETITIA
Good for joy, present or to come.		Good, exc. in war
		Sickly
	3	Ill
	4	Meanly good
	S	Excellently good
	6	Evil generally
	7	Indifferent
	8	Evil generally
	9	Very good
	10	Good rather in war than in peace
	11	Good in all
	12	Evil generally

FORTUNA MAJOR		TRISTITIA	
Good for gain in things where a person has hopes to win.		Good. save in secrecy	
	2	Good, save in sad things	
	3	Good in all	
	4	Good in all but melancholy	
	5	Very good in all	
	6	Very good, exc. for debauchery	
	7	Good in all	
	8	Moderately good	
	9	Very good	
	10	Exceeding good, to go to superiors	
	11	Very good	
	12	Good in all	

		TRISTITIA
		Med., but good for treasure and fortifying
		Med.. but good to fortify
		Evil in all
	4	EVII in all
	S	Very evil
	6	Evil, exc. for debauchery
	7	Evil, but in secrecy good
	8	Gd. for inheritance and magic only
	9	Evil, exc. for magic
	10	Evil. exc. for fortification
	11	Evil in all
	12	Evil. but good for magic and treasure

	PUELLA		ALBUS
Good in all demands, especially those relating to women.	1 Good, exc. in war	Good for profit and for entering into a place or undertaking.	1 Good for marriage; mercurial; peace
	2 Very good		2 Good in all
	3 Good		3 Very good
	4 But indifferent		4 Good, exc. in war
	5 V. good, but notice the aspects		5 Good
	6 Good, but esp. so for debauchery		6 Good in all
	7 Good, exc. for war		7 Good, exc. for war
	8 Good		8 Good
	9 Good for music, otherwise medium		9 A messenger brings letters
	10 Good for place		10 Excellent in all
	11 Good, and love of ladies		11 Very good
	12 Good in all		12 Marvellously good

	PUER		CONJUNCTIO
Evil in most demands, except those relating to war and love.	1 Indifferent; best in war	Good with good, and evil with evil. Recovery of things lost.	1 Good with good, evil with evil
	2 Good, but with trouble		2 Commonly good
	3 Good fortune		3 Good fortune
	4 Evil, exc. in war and love		4 Good, save for health. *Cf 8th* House's figure
	5 Medium good		5 Medium
	6 Medium		6 Good for immorality only
	7 Evil, save in war		7 Rather good
	8 Evil, exc. in love		8 Evil, death
	9 **Evil, exc. for war**		9 Medium good
	10 Evil rather; good for love and war, **else medium.**		10 **For love good, for sickness evil**
	11 Medium; good favour		11 Good in all
	12 Very good in all		12 Medium bad for prisoners

	RUBEUS		CARCER
is all that is good, and good in all that is evil.	1 Destroy the figure	General evil, delay, binding, stay, bar, restriction.	1 Evil except to fortify a place
	2 Evil in all		2 **Good in Saturnian questions,** otherwise evil
	3 Evil, exc. to let blood		3 Evil
	4 **Evil, exc. in war and fire**		4 Good, only for melancholy
	5 **Evil, exc. for sowing seed**		5 Receive a letter in three days; evil
	6 Evil, exc. for blood-letting		6 Very evil
	7 Evil, exc. for war and fire		7 Evil
	8 Evil		8 Very evil
	9 Very evil		9 Evil in all
	10 Dissolute, love, fire		10 Evil, save for hid treasure
	11 Evil, exc. blood-letting		11 Much anxiety
	12 Evil in all		12 Rather good

130

LIBERGAIAS

CAPUT DRACONIS		VrA	
With good, evil with evil; gives a good issue for gain. ○	1 Good in all 2 Good 3 Very good 4 Good, save in war 5 Very good 6 Good for immorality only 7 Good, esp. for peace 8 Good 9 Very good 10 Good in all 11 Good for the Church and ecclesiastical gain. 12 Not very good	Injurious to the goodness of other figs. generally, but gd for journeys & voyages	1 Evil, exc. for prison 2 Indifferent 3 Very good in all 4 Good in all, save love 5 Voyages good 6 Evil 7 Rather good, esp. for voyages 8 Evil 9 Indifferent; good for journeys 10 Good 11 Very good 12 Excellent

CAUDA DRACONIS		POPULUS	
Good with evil, and evil with good; good for loss, and for passing out of an affair.	1 Destroy the figure 2 Very evil 3 Evil in all 4 Good, esp. for conclusion of the matter 5 Very evil 6 Rather good 7 Evil, war, and fire 8 No good, exc. for magic 9 Good for science only; bad for journeys; robbery 10 Evil, save in works of fire 11 Evil, save for favours 12 Rather good	Sometimes good, sometimes bad; good with good, evil with evil.	Good for marriage Medium good Rather good than bad 4 Good in all but love S Good in mos! 6 Good 7 In war good, else medium 8 Evil 9 Look for letters 10 Good 11 Good in all n Very evil

CHAPTER VI

OF THE ESSENTIAL DIGNITIES OF THE FIGURES IN THE HOUSES; OF
THE ASPECTS OF THE HOUSES; AND OF THE FRIENDSHIP AND
EMNITY OF THE RULERS IN ASPECTS, ETC.

BY Essential Dignity is meant the strength of a figure when found in a particular House. A figure is therefore strongest in what is called its House; very strong in its Exaltation; strong in its Triplicity; very weak in its Fall; weakest of all in its Detriment. A figure is in its Fall when in a House opposite to that of its Exaltation; in is Detriment when opposite to its own House. The following list shows the Essential Dignities; that is to say, they follow the Dignities of their Ruling Planets, considering the twelve Houses of the scheme as answering to the twelve signs, thus: Asc. to ♈, 2 to ♉, 3 to ♊, &c., . . . 12 to ♓. Therefore ♂ figures will be strong in Asc. and weak in 7th and so on. *See* chapter I. for attribution of figures to planets.

⁙ is strong in Dignities of ♃ and ♀.

⸪ is strong in Dignities of ♄ and ♂.

TABLE OF ESSENTIAL DIGNITIES

—	House	Exaltation	Triplicity	Fall	Detriment
Asc.	☿ ☊ ⚴	☿ ♃	☿ ♃ ☽ ♅ ♄ ♀	♀ ♆	☉ ♀ ♈
2	☉ ♀ ♈	☊ ♊	♊ ♂ ☉ ♀ ♈	—	☿ ☊ ⚴
3	♀ ♆ ♄	♈	♀ ♆ ♅ ☊ ⚴	⚴	♅ ♃ ♈
4	♊ ♊	☿ ♃	☿ ☊ ⚴	☿ ☿	♀ ♆ ⚴
5	☿ ♃	—	☿ ♃ ☽ ♃ ♄	—	♀ ♆ ⚴
6	♅ ♓	♅ ♓	♊ ☿ ☉ ♀ ♈	☉ ♀	♅ ♃ ♈
7	☉ ♀ ♈	♀ ♆	♀ ♆ ♅ ☊ ⚴	☿ ♃	☿ ☊ ⚴

—	HOUSE	EXALTATION	TRIPLICITY	FALL	DETRIMENT
8	 ♄ ♅ ♃	——	 ♄ ♅ ♃	♊ ♍	 ☽ ♀ ♈
9	 ☿ ♁ ♈	♃	 ♃ ♄ ☽ ♁ ♈	♈	 ♄ ♅ ♃
10	 ♄ ♅ ♃	♄ ♅	 ♊ ♍ ☽ ♀ ♈	☽ ♁	♊ ♍
11	 ♄ ♅ ♃	——	 ♄ ♅ ☽ ♃ ♃	——	♀ ♁
12	 ☿ ♁ ♈	☽ ♀	 ♄ ♅ ♃	♂ ☿	♅ ☿

THE ASPECTS OF THE HOUSES

The Asc. is aspected by 11, 10, 9 (as ✶ □ and △ Dexter and by 3, 4, 5 . . . Sinister, and has 7 in opposition.

The Dexter aspect is that which is *contrary* to the natural order of the Houses; it is stronger than the Sinister. So for other Houses. Figures have Friends and Enemies:— ♄ : ♃ ☉ ☿ ☽ Friends; ♂ ♀ Enemies. ♃ : ♄ ☉ ♀ ☿ ☽; and ♂. ♂ : ♀ ; and ☽ ♄ ☉ ☿. ☉ : ♃ ☉ ♀ ☿ ☽; and ♄. ♀ : ♃ ☉ ♂ ☿; and ♄. ☿ : ♄ ♃ ☉ ♀ ☽; and ♂. ☽ : ♃ ☉ ♀ ☿; and ♄ and ♂.

Also figures of △ are sympathetic with those of △, friendly with △ and ▽; hostile to ▽.

So ▽ symp. ▽, friendly △ and ▽, and host. △ : △ symp △, friendly △ and ▽, and host. ▽. ▽ symp. ▽, friendly ▽ and △, and host. △. Again, sign figures are friends to those ✶ or △, and hostile to those □ or in ☍.

CHAPTER VII

OF THE GENERAL METHOD OF JUDGING A FIGURE

REMEMBER always that if;•; or °f fall in the Ascendant, the figure is not fit for judgement. Destroy it instantly, and erect a new figure not less than two hours afterwards.

Your figure being thoroughly arranged as on p. 6, note first to what House the demand belongs. Then look for Witnesses and Judge in their special table, and see what is said under the head of the demand. Put this down. Note next what figure falls into the House required (if it spring into other Houses, these too should be considered); *e.g.* in a question of money stolen, if the figure in 2nd be also in 6th it might show the thief to be a servant in the house. Look next in the Table of Figures in the Houses, and see what the figure signifies in the especial House under consideration. Put this down also. Then by the Table of Aspects (p. 20) note down the figures* □ *t:.* and *cf*, putting good on one side, evil on the other; noting also the strength or weakness, friendliness or hostility to the figure of the House required, of these figures. Then add the meaning of the figure in the 4th, to signify the end of the matter. It may also assist you to form a Reconciler from the figure in the House required and the Judge, noting what figure results and whether it harmonises with one or both by nature (p. 20). Now consider all you have written, and according to the balance of Good and Evil, form your final judgement. Consider also always in money questions where the Part of Fortune falls.

Take, *e.g.*, the figure on p. 6, and form a judgement for loss of money in business therefrom.

Table of Witnesses and Judge say: Moderate.

In 2nd is:). Evil, showing obstacle, delay.

Part of Fortune EB is in Ase. with :::, showing loss through Querent's own blunders.

:) springs into no other Houses; .•. this does not affect the question.

The figures * and A of 2nd are X, :\ =:=, and :::, all good figures and friendly in nature = Well-intentioned help of friends.

The figures □ and J' are :=:, :=:, :-:, which are not hostile to :); therefore shows opposition not great.

The figure in the 4th is l:, which shows a good end, but with anxiety.

Forming a Reconciler we get i: again, a sympathetic figure but denoting delay= Delay, but helping Querent's wishes.

Adding all together-

1. Medium.
2. Evil and obstacles, delay;
3. Loss through Querent's self;
4. Strength for evil, medium only;
5. Well-intentioned aid of friends;
6. Not much opposition from enemies.
7. Ending good, but with anxiety;
8. Delay, but helping Querent's wishes-

we formulate this judgement:

That the Querent's loss in business has been principally owing to his own mismanagement; that he will have a long and hard struggle, but will meet with help from friends; that his obstacles will gradually give way; and that after much anxiety he will eventually recoup himself for his previous losses.

*** ***** ***

LIBER
COLLEGII
SANCTI

SVB FIGVRÂ

CLXXXV

BEING THE TASKS
OF THE GRADES
AND THEIR OATHS PROPER TO LIBER
XIII.

THE PUBLICATIONS

OF THE

A∴A∴

IN CLASS D

FROM

A TO G

V

A∴A∴

*Publication in
Class D*

A∴A∴

Publication in Class D.

Imprimatur.

D.D.S. Præmonstrator.

Date. . . . . No. . . . .

A∴A∴

The Task of a Probationer

0. Let any person be received by a Neophyte, the latter being responsible to his Zelator.

1. The period of Probation shall be at least one year.

2. The aspirant to the A∴A∴ shall hear the Lection (Liber LXI) and this note of his office; IF HE WILL, shall then procure the robe of a Probationer; shall choose with deep forethought and intense solemnity a motto.

3. On reception he shall receive the robe, sign the form provided and repeat the oath as appointed, and receive the First Volume of the Book.

4. He shall commit a chapter of Liber LXV to memory; and furthermore, he shall study the Publications of the A∴A∴ in Class B, and apply himself to such practices of Scientific Illuminism as seemeth him good.

5. Beside all this, he shall perform any tasks that the A∴A∴ may see fit to lay upon him. Let him be mindful that the word Probationer is no idle term, but that the Brothers will in many a subtle way prove him, when he knoweth it not.

6. When the sun shall next enter the sign under which he hath been received, his initiation may be granted unto him. He shall keep himself free from all other engagements for one whole week from that date.

7. He may at any moment withdraw from his association with the A∴A∴ simply notifying the Neophyte who introduced him.

8. He shall everywhere proclaim openly his connection with the A∴A∴ and speak of It and Its principles (even so little as he understandeth) for that mystery is the enemy of truth.

> One month before the completion of his year, he shall deliver a copy of the record to the Neophyte introducing, and repeat to him his chosen chapter of Liber LXV.

9. He shall hold himself chaste, and reverent toward his body, for that the ordeal of initiation is no light one. This is of peculiar importance in the last two months of his Probation.

10. Thus and not otherwise may he attain the great reward, YEA, MAY HE ATTAIN THE GREAT REWARD!

Liberty
Power
Destiny

Life
Putrefaction
Death

The Seal
of
V.V.V.V.V.
$8°=3°$

The Seal
of
O.S.V.
$6°=5°$

The Seal
of
D.D.S.
$7°=4°$

A∴A∴

The Oath of a Probationer

I, _____, being of sound mind and body, on this __ day of _____ [An __ O in _____ ° of _____] dohereby resolve: in the Presence of _____, a Neophyte of the A∴A∴. To prosecute the Great Work: which is, to obtain a scientific knowledge of the nature and powers of my own being.

May the *A∴A∴* crown the work, lend me of Its wisdom in the work, enable me to understand the work!

Reverence, duty, sympathy, devotion, assiduity, trust do I bring to the *A∴A∴* and in one year from this date may I be admitted to the knowledge and conversation of the *A∴A∴*!

Witness my hand _____ __

Motto _____

The Seal
of
N.S.F.
$5°=6°$

Love
Passion
Debauch

Light
Perception
Darkness

142

A∴A∴

Publication in Class D.

B.

The Task of a Neophyte

0. Let any Probationer who has accomplished his task to the satisfaction of the A∴A∴ be instructed in the proper course of procedure: which is:—Let him read through this note of his office, and sign it, paying the sum of One Guinea for Liber VII which will be given him on his initiation, and One Guinea for this Portfolio of Class D publications, B-G. Let him obtain the robe of a Neophyte, and entrust the same to the care of his Neophyte.

> He shall choose a new motto with deep forethought and intense solemnity, as expressing the clearer consciousness of his Aspiration which the year's Probation has given him.

> Let him make an appointment with his Neophyte at the pleasure of the latter for the ceremony of Initiation.

1. The Neophyte shall not proceed to the grade of Zelator in less than eight months; but shall hold himself free for four days for advancement at the end of that period.

2. He shall pass the four tests called the Powers of the Sphinx.

3. He shall apply himself to understand the nature of his Initiation.

4. He shall commit to memory a chapter of Liber VII; and furthermore, he shall study and practice Liber O in all its branches: also he shall begin to study Liber H and some one commonly accepted method of divination. He will further be examined in his power of Journeying in the Spirit Vision.

5. Beside all this, he shall perform any tasks that his Zelator in the name of the A∴A∴ and by its authority may see fit to lay upon him. Let him be mindful that the word Neophyte is no idle term, but that in many a subtle way the new nature will stir within him, when he knoweth it not.

6. When the sun shall next enter the sign 240° to that under which he hath been received, his advancement may be granted unto him. He shall keep himself free from all other engagements for four whole days from that date.

7. He may at any moment withdraw from his association with the A∴A∴, simply notifying the Zelator who introduced him.

8. He shall everywhere proclaim openly his connection with the A∴A∴ and speak of It and Its principles (even so little as he understandeth) for that mystery is the enemy of truth.

Furthermore, he shall construct the magic Pentacle, according to the instruction in Liber A.

One month before the completion of his eight months, he shall deliver a copy of his Record to his Zelator, pass the necessary tests, and repeat to him his chosen chapter of Liber VII.

9. He shall in every way fortify his body according to the advice of his Zelator, for that the ordeal of advancement is no light one.

10. Thus and not otherwise may he attain the great reward, YEA, MAY HE ATTAIN THE GREAT REWARD!

The Oath of a Neophyte

I, _____ (old motto), being of sound mind and body, and prepared, on this ____ day of _____ [An ____ Sun in _____ ° of _____] do hereby resolve:in the Presence of _____, a Zelator of the A∴A∴: To prosecute the Great Work: which is, to obtain control of the nature and powers of my own being.

Further, I promise to observe zeal in service to the Probationers under me, and to deny myself utterly on their behalf.

May the A∴A∴ crown the work, lend me of Its wisdom in the work, enable me to understand the work!

Reverence, duty, sympathy, devotion, assiduity, trust do I bring to the A∴A∴ and in eight months from this date may I be admitted to the knowledge and conversation of the A∴A∴!

Witness my hand [old motto] _____

New Motto _____

A∴A∴

Publication in Class D.

C.

The Task of a Zelator

0. Let any Neophyte who has accomplished his task to the satisfaction of the A∴A∴ be instructed in the proper course of procedure: which is:—

> Let him read through this note of his office, and sign it, paying the sum of Three Guineas for the volume containing Liber CCXX, Liber XXVII and Liber DCCCXIII, which will be given him on his initiation.

> Let him cause the necessary addition to be made to his Neophyte's robe, and entrust the same to the care of his Zelator.

> Let him make an appointment with his Zelator at the pleasure of the latter for the ceremony of initiation.

1. The Zelator shall proceed to the grade of Practicus at any time that authority confers it.

2. He shall pass Examinations in Liber E, Posture and Breathing. He shall have attained complete success in the former, i.e., the chosen posture shall be perfectly steady and easy; and attained the second stage in the latter, i.e., automatic rigidity.

3. He shall further show some acquaintance with and experience of the meditations given in Liber HHH. And in this his Record shall be his witness.

4. He shall commit to memory a chapter of Liber CCXX; he shall pass examinations in Liber HHH.

5. Beside all this, he shall apply himself to work for the A∴A∴ upon his own responsibility.

> Let him be mindful that the word Zelator is no idle term; but that a certain Zeal will be inflamed within him, why he knoweth not.

6. When authority confers the grade, he shall rejoice therein; but beware, for that is his first departure from the middle pillar of the Tree of Life.

7. He may at any moment withdraw from his association with the A∴A∴, simply notifying the Practicus who introduced him.

> Yet let him remember that being entered thus far upon the Path, he cannot escape it, and return to the world, but must ultimate either in the City of the Pyramids or the lonely towers of the Abyss.

8. He shall everywhere proclaim openly his connection with the A∴A∴ and speak of It and Its principles (even so little as he understandeth) for that mystery is the enemy of truth. Furthermore, he shall construct the magic Dagger, according to the instruction in Liber A.

> One month after his admission to the Grade he shall go to his Practicus, pass the necessary tests, and repeat to him his chosen chapter of Liber CCXX.

9. He shall in every way establish perfect control of his Automatic Consciousness according to the advice

of his Practicus, for that the ordeal of advancement is no light one.

10. Thus and not otherwise may he attain the great reward, YEA, MAY HE ATTAIN THE GREAT REWARD!

The Oath of a Zelator

I, _____ (motto), being of sound mind and body, and prepared, on this ____ day of _____ [An ____ Sun in _____ ° of _____] do hereby resolve: in the Presence of _____, a Practicus of the A∴A∴: To prosecute the Great Work: which is, to obtain control of the foundations of my own being.

Further, I promise to observe zeal in service to the Neophytes under me, and to deny myself utterly on their behalf.

May the A∴A∴ crown the work, lend me of Its wisdom in the work, enable me to understand the work!

Reverence, duty, sympathy, devotion, assiduity do I bring to the A∴A∴ and right soon may I be admitted to the knowledge and conversation of the A∴A∴!

Witness my hand [motto] _____

This paper is to be returned to the Chancellor of the A∴A∴ through the Philosophus admitting.

A∴A∴

Publication in Class D.

D.

The Task of a Practicus

0. Let any Zelator be appointed by authority to proceed to the grade of Practicus.

Let him then read through this note of his office, and sign it.

Let him cause the necessary addition to be made to his Zelator's robe.

Let him make an appointment with his Practicus at the pleasure of the latter for the conferring of advancement.

1. The Practicus shall proceed to the grade of Philosophus at any time that authority confers it.

2. He shall pass examinations in Liber DCCLXXVII, the Qabalah, and the Sepher Sephiroth.

He shall attain complete success in Liber III, Cap I.

3. He shall further show some acquaintance with and experience of his chosen method of divination. Yet he shall be his own judge in this matter.

4. He shall commit to memory Liber XXVII and pass examinations in the Ritual and meditation practice given in Liber XVI. Further, he shall pass the meditation practice S.S.S., in Liber HHH.

5. Besides all this, he shall apply himself to a way of life wholly suited to the Path.

Let him remember that the word Practicus is no idle term, but that Action is the equilibrium of him that is in the House of Mercury, who is the Lord of Intelligence.

6. When authority confers the grade, he shall rejoice therein; but beware, for that that is his second departure from the middle pillar of the Tree of Life.

7. Let him not venture while a member of the grade of Practicus to attempt to withdraw from his association with the A∴A∴

8. He shall everywhere proclaim openly his connection with the A∴A∴ and speak of It and Its principles (even so little as he understandeth) for that mystery is the enemy of truth.

Furthermore, he shall construct the magic Cup, according to the instruction in Liber A.

One month after his admission to the Grade, he shall go to his Practicus, pass the necessary tests, and repeat to him Liber XXVII.

9. He shall in every way establish perfect control of his wit according to the advice of his Philosophus, for that the ordeal of advancement is no light one.

10. Thus and not otherwise may he attain the great reward, YEA, MAY HE ATTAIN THE GREAT REWARD!

The Oath of a Practicus

I, _____ (motto), being of sound mind and body, and prepared, on this ___ day of _____ [An ___ Sun in _____ ° of _____] do hereby resolve: in the Presence of _____, a Philosophus of the A∴A∴: To prosecute the Great Work: which is, to obtain control of the vacillations of my own being.

Further, I promise to observe zeal in service to the Zelatores under me, and to deny myself utterly on their behalf.

May the A∴A∴ crown the work, lend me of Its wisdom in the work, enable me to understand the work!

Reverence, duty, sympathy, devotion do I bring to the A∴A∴ and right soon may I be admitted to the knowledge and conversation of the A∴A∴!

Witness my hand [motto] _____

This paper is to be returned to the Chancellor of the A∴A∴ through the Dominus Liminis admitting.

A∴A∴

Publication in Class D.

E.

The Task of a Philosophus

0. Let any Practicus be appointed by authority to proceed to the grade of Philosophus.

Let him then read through this note of his office, and sign it.

Let him cause the necessary addition to be made to his Practicus' robe.

Let him make an appointment with his Philosophus at the pleasure of the latter for the conferring of advancement.

1. The Philosophus shall proceed to the grade of Dominus Liminis at any time that authority confers it.

2. He shall pass examinations in Liber CLXXV and in Construction and Consecration of Talismans and in Evocation. Yet in this matter he shall be his own judge.

He shall moreover attain complete success in Liber III, Cap. II.

Further, he shall apply himself to study and practice the meditations given in Liber V.

3. He shall further show some acquaintance with and experience of Liber O, Caps. V, VI. Whereof his Record shall be his witness.

4. He shall commit to memory a chapter of Liber DCCCXIII.

5. Besides all this, he shall make constant and profound reflections upon the Path.

Let him remember that the word Philosophus is no idle term, but that Philosophy is the Equilibrium of him that is in the house of Venus that is the Lady of Love.

6. When the title of Dominus Liminis is conferred upon him, let him rejoice exceedingly therein; but beware, for that it is but the false veil of the moon that hangs beneath the Sun.

7. Let him not venture while a member of the grade of Philosophus to attempt to withdraw from his association with the A∴A∴

8. He shall everywhere proclaim openly his connection with the A∴A∴ and speak of It and Its principles (even so little as he understandeth) for that mystery is the enemy of truth.

Furthermore, he shall construct the magic Wand, according to the instruction in Liber A.

One month after his admission to the Grade, he shall go to his Dominus Liminis, pass the necessary tests, and repeat to him his chosen chapter of Liber DCCCXIII.

9. He shall in every way establish perfect control of his devotion according to the advice of his Dominus Liminis, for that the ordeal of advancement is no light one.

10. Thus and not otherwise may he attain the great reward, YEA, MAY HE ATTAIN THE GREAT REWARD!

The Oath of a Philosophus

I, _____ (motto), being of sound mind and body, and prepared, on this ____ day of _____ [An ____ Sun in _____ ° of _____] do hereby resolve: in the Presence of _____, a Dominus Liminis of the A∴A∴. To prosecute the Great Work: which is, to obtain control of the attractions and repulsions of my own being.

Further, I promise to observe zeal in service to the Practici under me, and to deny myself utterly on their behalf.

May the A∴A∴ crown the work, lend me of Its wisdom in the work, enable me to understand the work!

Reverence, duty, sympathy do I bring to the A∴A∴ and right soon may I be admitted to the knowledge and conversation of the A∴A∴!

Witness my hand [motto] _____

157

This paper is to be returned to the Chancellor of the A∴A∴ through the Adeptus Minor admitting.

A∴A∴

Publication in Class D.

F.

The Task of a Dominus Liminis

0. Let any Philosophus be appointed by authority a Dominus Liminis.

> Let him read through this note of his office and sign it.

> Let him cause the necessary addition to be made to his Philosophus' robe.

> Let him receive Liber Mysteriorum.

> Let him make an appointment with his Dominus Liminis at the pleasure of the latter for the conferring of advancement.

1. The Dominus Liminis shall proceed to the Grade of Adeptus Minor at any time that authority confers it.

2. He shall pass examination in Liber III, Cap. III.

3. He shall meditate on the diverse knowledge and Power that he has acquired, and harmonize it perfectly. And in this matter he shall be judged by the Præmonstrator of the A∴A∴

4. He shall accept an office in a Temple of Initiation, and commit to memory a part appointed by the Imperator of the A∴A∴

5. Besides all this, he shall abide on the Threshold. Let him remember that the word Dominus Liminis is no idle term, but that his mastery will often be disputed, when he knoweth it not.

6. When at last he hath attained to the grade of Adeptus Minor, let him humble himself exceedingly.

7. He may at any moment withdraw from his association with the A∴A∴ simply notifying the Adept who introduced him.

8. He shall everywhere proclaim openly his connection with the A∴A∴ and speak of It and Its principles (even so little as he understandeth) for that mystery is the enemy of truth.

> Furthermore, he shall construct the magic Lamp, according to the instruction in Liber A.

> Six months after his admission to the Grade, he shall go to his Adeptus Minor, pass the necessary tests, and repeat to him his appointed part in the Temple of Initiation.

9. He shall in every way establish perfect control of his intuition, according to the advice of his Adeptus Minor, for that the ordeal of advancement is no light one.

10. Thus and not otherwise may he attain the great reward, YEA, MAY HE ATTAIN THE GREAT REWARD!

The Oath of a Dominus Liminis

I, _____ (motto), being of sound mind and body, and prepared, on this ____ day of _____ [An ____ Sun in _____ ° of _____] do hereby resolve: in the Presence of _____, an Adeptus Minor of the A∴A∴ To prosecute the Great Work: which is, to obtain control of the aspirations of my own being.

Further, I promise to observe zeal in service to the Philosophi under me, and to deny myself utterly on their behalf.

May the A∴A∴ crown the work, lend me of Its wisdom in the work, enable me to understand the work!

Reverence, duty, sympathy do I bring to the A∴A∴ and right soon may I be admitted to the knowledge and conversation of the A∴A∴!

Witness my hand [motto] _____

A∴A∴

Publication in Class D.

G.

The Task of an Adeptus Minor

Let the Adeptus Minor attain to the Knowledge and Conversation of his Holy Guardian Angel.

The Oath of an Adeptus Minor

I, _____ (motto), being of sound mind and body, and prepared, on this ____ day of _____ [An ____ Sun in _____ ° of _____] do hereby resolve: in the Presence of _____, an Adeptus of the A∴A∴: To prosecute the Great Work: which is, to attain to the knowledge and conversation of the Holy Guardian Angel.

May the A∴A∴ crown the work, lend me of Its wisdom in the work, enable me to understand the work!

Reverence, duty, sympathy do I bring to the A∴A∴ and here and now may I be admitted to the knowledge and conversation of the A∴A∴!

Witness my h

162

LIBER HHH

SVB FIGVRÂ

CCCXLI

CONTINET CAPITVLA TRIA :

MMM,

AAA, ET

SSS

V

A∴A∴

Publication in Class D

.

"Sunt duo modi per quos homo fit Deus: Tohu et Bohu.

"Mens quasi flamma surgat, aut quasi puteus aquæ quiescat.

"Alteri modi sunt tres exempli, qui illis extra limine collegii sancti dati sunt.

"In hoc primo libro sunt Aquæ Contemplationis."

Two are the methods of becoming God: the Upright and the Averse. Let the Mind become as a flame, or as a well of still water.

Of each method are three principal examples given to them that are without the Threshold.

In this first book are written the Reflexions.[1]

"Sunt tres contemplationes quasi halitus in mente humana abysso inferni. Prima, Νεκρος; secunda, Πυραμις; tertia, Φαλλος vocatur. Et hæ reflexiones aquaticæ sunt trium enthusiasmorum, Apollonis, Dionysi, Veneris.

"Total stella est Nechesh et Messiach, nomen hyha cum hwhy conjunctum."

There are three contemplations as it were breaths in the human mind, that is the Abyss of Hell: the first is called Νεκρος,[2] the second Πυραμις,[3] and the third Φαλλος.[4] These are the watery reflexions of the three enthusiasms; those of Apollo, Dionysus, and Aphrodite.[5]

The whole star is Nechesh and Messiach, the name hyha joined with hwhy.[6]

I

M M M

"I remember a certain holy day in the dusk of the Year, in the dusk of the Equinox of Osiris, when I first beheld thee visibly; when first the dreadful issue was fought out; when the Ibis-headed one charmed away the strife. I remember thy first kiss, even as a maiden should. Nor in the dark byways was there another: thy kisses abide."—LIBER LAPIDIS LAZULI. VII. 3.

0. Be seated in thine āsana, wearing the robe of a Neophyte, the hood drawn.

1. It is night, heavy and hot; there are no stars. Not one breath of wind stirs the surface of the sea, that is thou. No fish play in thy depths.

2. Let a Breath rise and ruffle the waters. This also thou shalt feel playing upon thy skin. It will disturb thy meditation twice or thrice, after which thou shouldst have conquered in. But unless thou first feel it, that Breath hath not arisen.

3. Next, the night is riven by the lightning-flash. This also shalt thou feel in thy body, which shall shiver and leap with the shock, and that also must both be suffered and overcome.

4. After the lightning-flash, resteth in the zenith a minute point of light. And this light shall radiate until a right cone be established upon the sea, and it is day. With this thy body shall be rigid, automatically; and this shalt thou let endure, withdrawing thyself into

166

thine heart in the form of an upright Egg of blackness; and therein shalt thou abide for a space.

5. When all this is perfectly and easily performed at will, let the aspirant figure to himself a struggle with the whole force of the Universe. In this he is only saved by his minuteness.

But in the end he is overthrown by Death, who covers him with a black cross.

Let his body fall supine with arms outstretched.

6. So lying, let him aspire fervently unto the Holy Guardian Angel.

7. Now let him resume his former posture.

Two-and-twenty times shall he figure to himself that he is bitten by a serpent, feeling even in his body the poison thereof. And let each bite be healed by an eagle or hawk, spreading its wings above his head, and dropping thereupon an healing dew. But let the last bite be so terrible a pang at the nape of the neck that he seemeth to die, and let the healing dew be of such virtue that he leapeth to his feet.

8. Let there be now placed within his egg a red cross, then a green cross, then a golden cross, then a silver cross; or those things which these shadow forth. Herein is silence; for he that hath rightly performed the meditation will understand the inner meaning hereof, and it shall serve as a test of himself and his fellows.

9. Let him now remain in the Pyramid or Cone of Light, as an Egg, but no more of blackness.

10. Then let his body be in the position of the Hanged Man, and let him aspire with all his force unto the Holy Guardian Angel.

11. The grace having been granted unto him, let him partake mystically of the Eucharist of the Five Elements and let him proclaim Light in Extension; yea, let him proclaim Light in Extension.[7]

II

A A A

"These loosen the swathings of the corpse; these unbind the feet of Osiris, so that the flaming God may rage through the firmament with his fantastic spear."—LIBER LAPIDIS LAZULI. VII. 15, 16.

0. Be seated in thine āsana, or recumbent in śavāsana,[8] or in the position of the dying Buddha.

1. Think of thy death; imagine the various the various diseases that may attack thee, or accidents overtake thee. Picture the process of death, applying always to thyself. (A useful preliminary practice is to read text-books of Pathology, and to visit museums and dissecting-rooms.)

2. Continue this practice until death is complete; follow the corpse through the stages of embalming, wrapping and burial.

3. Now imagine a divine breath entering thy nostrils.

4. Next, imagine a divine light enlightening the eyes.

5. Next, imagine the divine voice awakening the ears.

6. Next, imagine a divine kiss imprinted on the lips.

7. Next, imagine the divine energy informing the nerves and muscles of the body, and concentrate on the phenomenon which will already have been observed in 3, the restoring of the circulation.

8. Last, imagine the return of the reproductive power; and employ this to the impregnation of the Egg of light in which man is bathed.

9. Now represent to thyself that this egg is the Disk of the Sun, setting in the west.

10. Let it sink into blackness, borne in the bark of heaven, upon the back of the holy cow Hathor. And it may be that thou shalt hear the moaning thereof.

11. Let it become blacker than all blackness. And in this meditation thou shalt be utterly without fear, for that the blackness that will appear unto thee is a thing dreadful beyond all comprehension.

> And it shall come to pass that if thou hast well and properly performed this meditation that on a sudden thou shalt hear the drone and booming of a Beetle.

12. Now then shall the Blackness pass, and with rose and gold shalt thou arise in the East, with the cry of an Hawk resounding in thine ear. Shrill shall it be and harsh.

13. At the end shalt thou rise and stand in the midheaven, a globe of glory. And therewith shall arise the mighty Sound that holy men have likened unto the roaring of a Lion.

14. Then shalt thou withdraw thyself from the Vision, gathering thyself into the divine form of Osiris upon his throne.

15. Then shalt thou repeat audibly the cry of triumph of the god rearisen, as it shall have been given unto thee by the Superior.[9]

16. And this being accomplished, thou mayest enter again into the Vision, that thereby shalt be perfect in thee.

17. After this shalt thou return into the body, and give thanks unto the Most High God IAIDA; yea, unto the Most High God IAIDA.[10]

18. Mark well that this operation should be performed if it be possible in a place set apart and consecrated to the Works of the Magic of Light. Also that the Temple should be ceremonially open as thou hast knowledge and skill to perform, and that at the end thereof the closing should be most carefully accomplished.

> But in the preliminary practice it is enough if thou cleanse thyself by ablution, by robing, and by the rituals of the Pentagram and Hexagram.

> 0-2 should be practiced at first, until some realisation is obtained; and the practice should always be followed by a divine invocation of Apollo or of Isis or of Jupiter or of Serapis.

> Next, after a swift summary of 0-2, practise 3-7.

> , This being mastered, add 8.

> Then add 9-13.

> Then being prepared and fortified, well fitted for the work, perform the whole meditation at one time. And let this be continued until perfect success be attained therein. For this is a mighty meditation and holy, having power even upon Death; yea, having power even upon Death.[11]

(Note by Fra. O.M. At any time during this meditation, the concentration may bring about

samādhi. This is to be feared and shunned, more than any other breaking of control, for that it is the most tremendous of the forces which threaten to obsess. There is also some danger of acute delirious melancholia at point 1.)

III

S S S

*"Thou art a beautiful thing, whiter than a
woman in the column of this vibration.*

*"I shoot up vertically like an arrow, and
become that Above.*

"But it is death, and the flame of the pyre.

*"Ascend in the flame of the pyre, O my soul!
Thy God is like the cold emptiness of the
utmost heaven, into which thou radiatest thy
little light.*

*"When Thou shalt know me, O empty God, my
flame shall utterly expire in Thy great
N.O.X."—LIBER LAPIDIS LAZULI. I. 36-40.*

0. Be seated in thine āsana, preferably the
Thunderbolt. It is essential that the spine be vertical.

1. In this practice the cavity of the brain is the Yoni;
the spinal cord is the Lingam.

2. Concentrate thy thought of adoration in the brain.

3. Now begin to awake the spine in this manner.
Concentrate thy thought of thyself in the base of the
spine, and move it up gradually a little at a time.

> By this means thou wilt become conscious of the
> spine, feeling each vertebra as a separate entity.
> This must be achieved most fully and perfectly
> before the further practice is begun.

4. Next, adore the brain as before, but figure to
thyself its content as infinite. Deem it to be the womb
of Isis, or the body of Nuit.

5. Next, identify thyself with the base of the spine as before, but figure to thyself its energy as infinite. Deem it to be the phallus of Osiris, or the being of Hadit.

6. These two concentrations 4 and 5 may be pushed to the point of samādhi. Yet lose not control of the will; let not samādhi be thy master herein.

7. Now then, being conscious both of the brain and the spine, and unconscious of all else, do thou imagine the hunger of the one for the other; the emptiness of the brain, the ache of the spine, even as the emptiness of space and the aimlessness of Matter. And if thou hast experience of the Eucharist in both kinds,[12] it shall aid thine imagination herein.

8. Let this agony grow until it be insupportable, resisting by will every temptation. Not until thine whole body is bathed in sweat, or it may be in sweat of blood, and until a cry of intolerable anguish is forced from thy closed lip, shalt thou proceed.

9. Now let a current of light, deep azure flecked with scarlet, pass up and down the spine, striking as it were upon thyself that art coiled at the base as a serpent.

> Let this be exceeding slow and subtle; and though it be accompanied with pleasure, resist; and though it be accompanied with pain, resist.

10. This shalt thou continue until thou art exhausted, never relaxing the control. Until thou canst perform this one section 9 during a whole hour, proceed not. And withdraw from the meditation by an act of will, passing into a gentle prānāyāma without kumbhakha, and meditating on Harpocrates, the silent and virginal God.

11. Then at last being well-fitted in body and mind, fixed in peace, beneath a favourable heaven of stars, at night, in calm and warm weather, mayst thou quicken the movement of the light until it be taken up by the brain and the spine, independently of thy will. If in this hour thou shouldst die, is it not written: "Blessed are the dead that die in the Lord"[13]? Yea, blessed are the dead that die in the Lord![14]

*** ***** ***

LIBER A
vel
ARMORUM
SVB FIGVRA CDXII

"... the obeah and the wanga; the work of the wand and the work of the sword; these he shall learn and teach." Liber AL, I, 37.

The Pantacle.

Take pure wax, or a plate of gold, silver-gilt or Electrum Magicum. The diameter shall be eight inches, and the thickness half an inch.

Let the Neophyte by his understanding and ingenium devise a symbol to represent the Universe.

Let his Zelator approve thereof.

Let the Neophyte engrave the same upon the plate with his own hand and weapon.

Let it when finished be consecrated as he hath skill to perform, and kept wrapped in silk of emerald green.

The Dagger.

Let the Zelator take a piece of pure steel, and beat it, grind it, sharpen it, and polish it, according to the art of the swordsmith.

Let him further take a piece of oak wood, and carve a hilt. The length shall be eight inches.

Let him by his understanding and ingenium devise a Word to represent the Universe.

Let his Practicus approve thereof.

Let the Zelator engrave the same upon his dagger with his own hand and instruments.

Let him further gild the wood of his hilt.

Let it when finished be consecrated as he hath skill to perform, and kept wrapped in silk of golden yellow.

The Cup.

Let the Practicus take a piece of Silver and fashion therefrom a cup. The height shall be 8 inches, and the diameter 3 inches.

Let him by his understanding and ingenium devise a Number to represent the Universe.

Let his Philosophus approve thereof.

Let the Practicus engrave the same upon his cup with his own hand and instrument.

Let it when finished be consecrated as he hath skill to perform, and kept wrapped in silk of azure blue.

The Baculum.

Let the Philosophus take a rod of copper, of length eight inches and diameter half an inch.

Let him fashion about the top a triple flame of gold.

Let him by his understanding and ingenium devise a Deed to represent the Universe.

Let his Dominus Liminis approve thereof.

Let the Philosophus perform the same in such a way that the Baculum may be partaker therein.

Let it when finished be consecrated as he hath skill to perform, and kept wrapped in silk of fiery scarlet.

The Lamp.

Let the Dominus Liminis take pure lead, tin, and quicksilver, with platinum, and, if need be, glass.

Let him by his understanding and ingenium devise a Magick Lamp that shall burn without wick or oil, being fed by the Aethyr.

This shall he accomplish secretly and apart, without asking the advice or approval of his Adeptus Minor.

Let the Dominus Liminis keep it when consecrated in the secret chamber of Art.

This then is that which is written: "Bring furnished with complete armour and armed, he is similar to the goddess."

And again, "I am armed, I am armed."

~

Liber OS ABYSMI

vel

DAATH

sub figura CDLXXIV

A∴A∴

Publication in Class B.

Imprimatur:

N. Fra A∴A∴

1. This book is the Gate of the Secret of the Universe.

2. Let the Exempt Adept procure the Prolegomena of Kant, and study it, paying special attention to the Antinomies.

3. Also Hume's doctrine of Causality in his "Enquiry."

4. Also Herbert Spencer's discussion of the three theories of the Universe in his "First Principles," Part I.

5. Also Huxley's Essays on Hume and Berkeley.

6. Also Crowley's Essays: Berashith, Time, The Soldier and the Hunchback, et cetera.

7. Also the "Logik" of Hegel.

8. Also the "Questions of King Milinda" and the Buddhist Suttas which bear on Metaphysic.

9. Let him also be accomplished in Logic. (Formal Logic, Keynes.) Further let him study any classical works to which his attention may be sufficiently directed in the course of his reading.

10. Now let him consider special problems, such as the Origin of the World, the Origin of Evil, Infinity, the Absolute, the Ego and the non-Ego, Freewill and Destiny, and such others as may attract him.

11. Let him subtly and exactly demonstrate the fallacies of every known solution, and let him seek a true solution by his right Ingenium.

12. In all this let him be guided only by clear reason, and let him forcibly suppress all other qualities such as Intuition, Aspiration, Emotion, and the like.

13. During these practices all forms of Magick Art and Meditation are forbidden to him. It is forbidden to him to seek any refuge from his intellect.

14. Let then his reason hurl itself again and again against the blank wall of mystery which will confront him.

15. Thus also following is it said, and we deny it not. At last automatically his reason will take up the practice, sua sponte, and he shall have no rest therefrom.

16. Then will all phenomena which present themselves to him appear meaningless and disconnected, and his own Ego will break up into a series of impressions having no relation one with the other, or with any other thing.

17. Let this state then become so acute that it is in truth Insanity, and let this continue until exhaustion.

18. According to a certain deeper tendency of the individual will be the duration of this state.

19. It may end in real insanity, which concludes the activities of the Adept during this present life, or by his rebirth into his own body and mind with the simplicity of a little child.

20. And then shall he find all his faculties unimpaired, yet cleansed in a manner ineffable.

21. And he shall recall the simplicity of the Task of the Adeptus Minor, and apply himself thereto with fresh energy in a more direct manner.

22. And in his great weakness it may be that for awhile the new Will and Aspiration are not puissant, yet being undisturbed by those dead weeds of doubt

and reason which he hath uprooted, they grow imperceptibly and easily like a flower.

23. And with the reappearance of the Holy Guardian Angel he may be granted the highest attainments, and be truly fitted for the full experience of the destruction of the Universe. And by the Universe We mean not that petty Universe which the mind of man can conceive, but that which is revealed to his soul in the Samadhi of Atmadarshana.

24. Thence may he enter into a real communion with those that are beyond, and he shall be competent to receive communication and instruction from Ourselves directly.

25. Thus shall We prepare him for the confrontation of Choronzon and the Ordeal of the Abyss, when we have received him into the City of the Pyramids.

26. So, being of Us, let the Master of the Temple accomplish that Work which is appointed. (In Liber CDXVIII. is an adequate account of this Ordeal and Reception. See also Liber CLVI. for the preparation.)

27. Also concerning the Reward thereof, of his entering into the Palace of the King's Daughter, and of that which shall thereafter befall, let it be understood of the Master of the Temple. Hath he not attained to Understanding? Yea, verily, hath he not attained to Understanding?

~

LIBER DCLXXI vel PYRAMIDOS

A Ritual of Self Initiation based upon the Formula of the Neophyte.

By Aleister Crowley

000. The Building of the Pyramid. *The Magus with Wand. On the Altar are incense, Fire, Bread, Wine, the Chain, the Scourge, the Dagger & the Oil. In his left hand the Bell he taketh.*

Hail! Asi! hail, Hoor-Apep! Let

The Silence speech beget! *Two strokes on Bell.*

Banishing Spiral Dance.

The Words against the Sons of Night

Tahuti speaketh in the Light.

Knowledge & Power, twin warriors, shake

The Invisible; they roll asunder

The Darkness; matter shines, a snake.

Sebek is smitten by the   thunder—

The Light breaks forth from Under.

He goes to the West, in the centre of the base of the Triangle of THOTH (Maim), ASI (Aleph), & HOOR (Shin).

O Thou, the Apex of the Plane,

With Ibis head & Phoenix Wand

And Wings of Night! Whose serpents strain

Thou in the Light & in the Night!

He lays the Wand, etc., on the Altar, uses the Scourge on his buttocks, cuts a cross with the Daggar upon his breast & tightens the Chain of the Bell about his forehead, saying:

The Lustral Water! Smite thy flood

Through me—Lymph, marrow & blood! *Annointing the Wounds, say*

The Fire Informing! Let the Oil

Balance, assain, assoil! *The Invoking Spiral Dance.*

So Life takes Fire from Death, & runs

Whirling amid the Suns.

Hail, Asi! Pace the Path, bind on

The girdle of the Starry One!

Sign of the Enterer: Homage to Thee, Lord of the Word!

Sign of Silence: Lord of Silence, Homage to Thee!

Repeat both Signs: Lord we adore Thee, still & stirred Beyond Infinity.

The Secret Word: MTzThBTzM—271 (Blue, Orange, Yellow-Green, Yellow, Orange, Blue)

For from the Silence of the Wand

Unto the Speaking of the Sword,

And back again to the Beyond,

This is the toil & the Reward.

This is the Path of HVA—Ho!

This is the Path of IAO. *Bell.*

Hail Asi! Hail, thou Wanded Wheel!

Alpha & Delta kissed & came

For five that feed the Flame. *Bell.*

Hail, Hoor-Apep! thou Sword of Steel!

Alpha & Delta & Epsilon

Met in the Shadow of the Pylon

And in Iota did proclaim

That tenfold core & crown of flame.

Hail, Hoor-Apep! Unspoken Name!

Thus is the Great Pyramid duly builded.

1. Initiation. *The Candidate still bound and hoodwinked. The First Pylon.*

I know not who I am; I know not whence I came;

I know not whither I go; I seek—but What I do not know!

I am blind & bound; but I have heard one cry

Ring through Eternity; Arise & follow me!

Asar Un-nefer! I invoke

The four-fold Horror of the Smoke.

Unloose the Pit! by the dread Word

Of Power—that Set-Typhon hath heard—

SAZAZSAZAZADANATASANSAZAZ

(Pronounce this backwards. But it is very dangerous. It opens up the Gates of Hell.)

The Fear of Darkness & of Death

The Fear of Water & of Fire

The Fear of the Chasm & the Chain

The Fear of Hell & the dead Breath.

The Fear of Him, the Demon dire

That on the Threshold of the Inane

Stands with his Dragon Fear to slay

The Pilgrim of the Way.

Thus I pass by with Force & Care,

Advance with Fortitude & Wit,

In the straight Path, or else Their Snare

Were surely Infinite. *The Passing of the Second Pylon.*

(Suit action to words.)

Asar! who clutches at my throat?

Who pins me down? Who stabs my heart?

I am unfit to pass within this Pylon of the Hall of Maat.

Rubric as above. (The Fear.....surely Infinite.)

The Lustral Water! Let thy flood

Cleanse me—lymph, marrow, & blood!

The Scourge, the Dagger & the Chain

Purge body, breast & brain!

The Fire Informing! Let the Oil

Balance, assain, assoil! *Still in corpse—position.*

For I am come with all this pain,

To ask admission to the Shrine.

I do not know why—I ask in vain—

Unless it be that I am Thine.

I am Mentu his truth-telling brother,

Who was Master of Thebes from my birth:—

O heart of me! heart of my mother!

O heart that I had upon the earth!

Stand not thou up against me as a witness!

Oppose me not, judge, in my quest!

Accuse me not now of unfitness

Before the great God, the dread Lord of the West!

(Change this part to your own motto. Work the scansion correctly.)

Speak fair words for OU MH. May he flourish

In the place of the weighing of hearts

By the marsh of the dead, where the crocodiles nourish

Their lives on the lost, where the Serpent upstarts.

—For though I be joined to the Earth,

In the Innermost Shrine of Heaven am I.

I was Master of Thebes from my birth;

Shall I die like a dog? Thou shalt not let me die,

But my Khu that the teeth of the crocodiles sever

Shall be mighty in heaven for ever & ever!

Yea! but I am a fool, a flutterer!

I am under the Shadow of the Wings!

Refrain "I am under," etc., after each accusation.

I am a liar & a sorcerer

I am so fickle that I scorn the bridle.

I am unchaste, voluptuous and idle.

190

I am a bully & a tyrant crass,

I am as dull & as stubborn as an ass;

I am untrusty, cruel & insane,

I am a fool & frivolous & vain.

I am a weakling & a coward; I cringe,

I am a catamite & cunnilinge.

I am a glutton, a besotted wight;

I am a satyr & a sodomite.

I am as changeful & selfish as the Sea.

I am a thing of vice & vanity.

I am not violent & I vaccilate,

I am a blind man & esmasculate.

I am a raging fire of wrath—no wiser!

I am a blackguard, spendthrift & a miser.

I am obscene & devious & null.

I am ungenerous & base & dull.

I am not marked with the white Flame of Breath.

I am a Traitor!—die the traitor's death!

This last raises Candidate erect.

Invoking Spiral Dance.

Rubric as before.

I am under the Shadow of the Wings.

Now let me pace the Path, bind on

The girdle of the Starry One!

Asar! k.t.l. *In Northwest.*

Soul—mastering Terror is thy name!

Lord of the Gods! Dread Lord of Hell! *See Horus.*

I am come. I fear Thee not. Thy flame

Is mine to weave my maiden spell!

I know Thee, & I pass Thee by.

For more that Thou am I!

Asar! k.t.l. (Rubric as usual.) In Southwest. See Isis.

Sorrow that eateth up the soul!

Dam of the Gods! The blue sky's Queen!

This is Thy Name. I come. Control

And Pass! I know Thee, Lady of Teeu!

know Thee & I pass Thee by.

For more than Thou am I!

*Asar! k.t.l. (Rubric as usual.) In East. See Thoth.
Silence*

Asar! k.t.l. (Rubric as usual.) See Nature.

I will not look upon thee more,

For Fatal is Thy Name. Begone!

False Phantom, thou shalt pass before

The frowning forehead of the Sun.

I know Thee; & I pass thee by.

For more that Thou am I. *Formulating Hexagram:*

Now Witness YE upon the Earth,

Spirit & Water & Red Blood!

Witness Above, bright Babe of Birth,

Spirit, & Father—that are God! *As babe in egg, being born.*

For Silence duly is begot

And Darkness duly brought to bed;

The Shroud is figured in my Thought,

The Inmost Light is on my head. *Unbind.*

Attack! I eat up the strong lions. I!

Sign of the Enterer:

Fear is on Seb, on them that dwell therein,

Behold the radient Vigour of the Lord! *Sign of Silence:*

Defense! I close the mouth of Sebek, ply

My fear on Nile, Asar that held not in!

Behold my radiant Peace, ye things abhorred

For see! The Gods have loosed mine hands:

Asar unfettered stands.

Hail, Asi, hail! Hoor-Apep cries—

Now I the Son of Man arise

And follow—dead where Asar lies!

Lies down in Sign of Hanged Man.

I guild my left foot with the Light.

I guild my Phallus with the Light.

I guild my right knee with the Light.

I guild my right foot with the Light.

I guild my left knee with the Light.

I guild my Phallus with the Light.

I guild my elbow with the Light.

I guild my navel with the Light.

I guild my heart wedge with the Light.

I guild my black throat with the Light.

I guild my forehead with the Light.

I guild my Phallus with the Light. *Rising in Sign Mulier:*

Asar Un-nefer! I am Thine,

Waiting Thy Glory in the shrine.

Thy bride, Thy virgin! Ah, my Lord.

Smite through the Spirit with Thy Sword!

Asar Un-nefer! rise in me,

The chosen catamite of Thee!

Come! Ah, come now! I wait, I wait,

Patient—impatient slave of Fate,

Bought by Thy glance—Come now! come now!

Touch & inform this burning brow.

Asar Un-nefer! in the shrine,

Make Thou me wholly Thine! *Remove hoodwink.*

I am Asar—worthy alone

To sit upon the Double Throne.

Attack is mine & mine defence.

And these are one. Arise, go hence!

For I am Master of my Fate,

Wholly Initiate. *The Secret Word.*

The Words are spoken duly. The deeds are duly done.

My soul is risen newly to greet the risen Sun.

Bell accordingly.

One! Four! Five! Ten! All Hail!

Hail!

One! Four! Five! Ten! All Hail!

Signs accordingly.

I give the sign that rends the Veil.

The sign that closes up the Veil.

2. The Sealing of the Pyramid.

Proceed as in the Building, unto the the word "Suns."

The Banishing Spiral Dance.

Now let mine hands unloose the sweet

And shining girdle of Nuit! *The Adorations & the Word.*

Then at the Altar.

Behold! the Perfect One hath said

Tried & found pure, a golden spoil.

These are my body's elements *Act accordingly.*

Incense & Wine & Fire & Bread

These I consume, true Sacraments,

For the Perfection of the Oil

For I am clothed about with flesh

And I am the Eternal Spirit.

I am the Lord that riseth fresh

From Death, whose glory I inherit

Since I partake with him. I am

The Manifestor of the Unseen.

Without me all the land of Khem

Is as if it had not been. *Proceed as in Building to end.*

Hail, Hoor! Hail, Asi! Hail, Tahuti! Hail,

Asar Un-nefer! through the rended Veil.

I am Thyself, with all Thy brilliance decked—

Khabs-Am-Pekht.

~

LIBER
DCCCXI

ENERGIZED
ENTHUSIASM

A NOTE ON
THEURGY

V

A∴A∴
Publication in Class C

LIBER DCCCXI

ENERGIZED ENTHUSIASM

A Note on Theurgy

V A∴A∴ Publication in Class B

I

I A O the supreme One of the Gnostics, the true God, is the Lord of this work. Let us therefore invoke Him by that name which the Companions of the Royal Arch blaspheme to aid us in the essay to declare the means which He has bestowed upon us!

II

The divine consciousness which is reflected and refracted in the works of Genius feeds upon a certain secretion, as I believe. This secretion is analogous to semen, but not identical with it. There are but few men and fewer women, those women being inevitably androgyne, who possess it at any time in any quantity. So closely is this secretion connected with the sexual economy that it appears to me at times as if it might be a by-product of that process which generates semen. That some form of this doctrine has been generally accepted is shown in the prohibitions of all religions. Sanctity has been assumed to depend on chastity, and chastity has nearly always been interpreted as abstinence. But I doubt whether the relation is so simple as this would imply; for example, I find in myself that manifestations of mental creative force always concur with some abnormal condition of the physical powers of generation. But it is not the case that long periods of chastity, on the one hand, or excess of orgies, on the other, are favourable to its manifestation, or even to its formation. I know myself, and in me it is extremely strong; its results are astounding. For example, I wrote Tannhäuser, complete from conception to execution, in sixty-seven consecutive hours. I was unconscious of the fall of nights and days, even after stopping; nor was there any reaction of fatigue. This work was written when I was twenty-four years old,

199

immediately on the completion of an orgie which would normally have tired me out. Often and often have I noticed that sexual satisfaction so-called has left me dissatisfied and unfatigued, and let loose the floods of verse which have disgraced my career. Yet, on the contrary, a period of chastity has sometimes fortified me for a great outburst. This is far from being invariably the case. At the conclusion of the K2 expedition, after five months of chastity, I did no work whatever, barring very few odd lyrics, for months afterwards. I may mention the year 1911. At this time I was living, in excellent good health, with the woman whom I loved. Her health was, however, variable, and we were both constantly worried. The weather was continuously fine and hot. For a period of about three months I hardly missed a morning; always on waking I burst out with a new idea which had to be written down. The total energy of my being was very high. My weight was 10 stone 8 lb., which had been my fighting weight when I was ten years younger. We walked some twenty miles daily through hilly forest. The actual amount of MSS. written at this time is astounding; their variety is even more so; of their excellence I will not speak.

Here is a rough list from memory; it is far from exhaustive: (1) Some dozen books of A∴A∴ instruction, including "Liber Astarte," and the Temple of Solomon the King for Equinox VII. (2) Short Stories: The Woodcutter; His Secret Sin. (3) Plays: His Majesty's Fiddler; Elder Eel; Adonis written straight off, one after the other; The Ghouls; Mortadello. (4) Poems: The Sevenfold Sacrament; A Birthday. (5) Fundamentals of the Greek Qabalah (involving the collection and analysis of several thousand words).

I think this phenomenon is unique in the history of literature. I may further refer to my second journey to Algeria, where my sexual life, though fairly full, had been unsatisfactory. On quitting Biskra, I was so full of ideas that I had to get off the train at El-Kantara, where I wrote "The Scorpion." Five or six poems were written on the way to Paris; "The Ordeal of Ida Pendragon" during my twenty-four hours' stay in Paris, and "Snowstorm" and "The Electric Silence" immediately on my return to England. To sum up, I can always trace a connection between my sexual condition and the condition of artistic creation, which is so close as to approach identity, and yet so loose that I cannot predicate a single important proposition. It is these considerations which give me pain when I am reproached by the ignorant with wishing to produce genius mechanically. I may fail, but my failure is a thousand times greater than their utmost success. I shall therefore base my remarks not so much on the observations which I have myself made, and the experiments which I have tried, as on the accepted classical methods of producing that energized enthusiasm which is the lever that moves God.

III

The Greeks say that there are three methods of discharging the genial secretion of which I have spoken. They thought perhaps that their methods tended to secrete it, but this I do not believe altogether, or without a qualm. For the manifestation of force implies force, and this force must have come from somewhere. Easier I find it to say "sub-consciousness" and "secretion" than to postulate an external reservoir, to extend my connotation of "man" than to invent "God." However, parsimony apart, I find it in my experience that it is useless to flog a tired horse. There are times when I am absolutely bereft of even one drop of this elixir. Nothing will restore it, neither rest in bed, nor drugs, nor exercise. On the other hand, sometimes when after a severe spell of work I have been dropping with physical fatigue, perhaps sprawling on the floor, too tired to move hand or foot, the occurrence of an idea has restored me to perfect intensity of energy, and the working out of the idea has actually got rid of the aforesaid physical fatigue, although it involved a great additional labour. Exactly parallel (nowhere meeting) is the case of mania. A madman may struggle against six trained athletes for hours, and show no sign of fatigue. Then he will suddenly collapse, but at a second's notice from the irritable idea will resume the struggle as fresh as ever. Until we discovered "unconscious muscular action" and its effects, it is rational to suppose such a man "possessed of a devil"; and the difference between the madman and the genius is not in the quantity but in the quality of their work. Genius is organized, madness chaotic.

Often the organization of genius is on original lines, and ill-balanced and ignorant medicine-men mistake it for disorder. Time has shown that Whistler and Gauguin "kept rules" as well as the masters whom they were supposed to be upsetting.

IV

The Greeks say that there are three methods of discharging the Leyden Jar of Genius. These three methods they assign to three Gods.

These three Gods are Dionysus, Apollo, Aphrodite. In English: wine, women and song. Now it would be a great mistake to imagine that the Greeks were recommending a visit to a brothel. As well condemn the High Mass at St. Peter's on the strength of having witnessed a Protestant revival meeting.

Disorder is always a parody of order, because there is no archetypal disorder that it might resemble.

Owen Seaman can parody a poet; nobody can parody Owen Seaman. A critic is a bundle of impressions; there is no ego behind it. All photographs are essentially alike; the works of all good painters essentially differ. Some writers suppose that in the ancient rites of Eleusis the High Priest publicly copulated with the High Priestess.

Were this so, it would be no more "indecent" than it is "blasphemous" for the priest to make bread and wine into the body and blood of God. True, the Protestants say that it is blasphemous; but a Protestant is one to whom all things sacred are profane, whose mind being all filth can see nothing in the sexual act but a crime or jest, whose only facial gestures are the sneer and the leer.

Protestantism is the excrement of human thought, and accordingly in Protestant countries art, if it exist at all, only exists to revolt. Let us return from this unsavoury allusion to our consideration of the methods of the Greeks.

V

Agree then that it does not follow from the fact that wine, woman and song make the sailor's tavern that these ingredients must necessarily concoct a hell-broth. There are some people so simple as to think that, when they have proved the religious instinct to be a mere efflorescence of the sex-instinct, they have destroyed religion. We should rather consider that the sailor's tavern gives him his only glimpse of heaven, just as the destructive criticism of the phallicists has only proved sex to be a sacrament. Consciousness, says the materialist, axe in hand, is a function of the brain. He has only re-formulated the old saying, "Your bodies are the temples of the Holy Ghost." Now sex is justly hallowed in this sense, that it is the eternal fire of the race. Huxley admitted that "some of the lower animalculæ are in a sense immortal," because they go on reproducing eternally by fission, and however often you divide x by 2 there is always something left. But he never seems to have seen that mankind is immortal in exactly the same sense, and goes on reproducing itself with similar characteristics through the ages, changed by circumstance indeed, but always identical in itself. But the spiritual flower of this process is that at the moment of discharge a physical ecstasy occurs, a spasm analogous to the mental spasm which meditation gives. And further, in the sacramental and ceremonial use of the sexual act, the divine consciousness may be attained.

VI

The sexual act being then a sacrament, it remains to consider in what respect this limits the employment of the organs. First, it is obviously legitimate to employ them for their natural physical purpose. But if it be allowable to use them ceremonially for a religious purpose, we shall find the act hedged about with many restrictions. For in this case the organs become holy. It matters little to mere propagation that men should be vicious; the most debauched roué might and almost certainly would beget more healthy children than a semi-sexed prude. So the so-called "moral" restraints are not based on reason; thus they are neglected. But admit its religious function, and one may at once lay down that the act must not be profaned. It must not be undertaken lightly and foolishly without excuse. It may be undertaken for the direct object of continuing the race. It may be undertaken in obedience to real passion; for passion, as its name implies, is rather inspired by a force of divine strength and beauty without the will of the individual, often even against it. It is the casual or habitual—what Christ called "idle"—use or rather abuse of these forces which constitutes their profanation. It will further be obvious that, if the act in itself is to be the sacrament in a religious ceremony, this act must be accomplished solely for the love of God. All personal considerations must be banished utterly. Just as any priest can perform the miracle of transubstantiation, so can any man, possessing the necessary qualifications, perform this other miracle, whose nature must form the subject of a subsequent discussion. Personal aims being destroyed, it is à fortiori necessary to neglect social and other similar considerations. Physical strength and beauty are necessary and desirable for æsthetic reasons, the attention of the worshippers being liable to distraction if the celebrants are ugly, deformed, or incompetent. I need hardly emphasize the necessity for the strictest self-control and concentration on their part. As it would be blasphemy to enjoy the gross taste of the wine of the sacrament, so must the celebrant suppress even the minutest manifestation of animal pleasure. Of the qualifying tests there is no necessity to speak; it is sufficient to say that the adepts have always known how to secure efficiency. Needless also to insist on a similar quality in the assistants; the sexual excitement must be suppressed and transformed into its religious equivalent.

VII

With these preliminaries settled in order to guard against foreseen criticisms of those Protestants who, God having made them a little lower than the Angels, have made themselves a great deal lower than the beasts by their consistently bestial interpretation of all things human and divine, we may consider first the triune nature of these ancient methods of energizing enthusiasm. Music has two parts; tone or pitch, and rhythm. The latter quality associates it with the dance, and that part of dancing which is not rhythm is sex. Now that part of sex which is not a form of the dance, animal movement, is intoxication of the soul, which connects it with wine. Further identities will suggest themselves to the student. By the use of the three methods in one the whole being of man may thus be stimulated. The music will create a general harmony of the brain, leading it in its own paths; the wine affords a general stimulus of its animal nature; and the sex-excitement elevates the moral nature of the man by its close analogy with the highest ecstasy. It remains, however, always for him to make the final transmutation. Unless he have the special secretion which I have postulated, the result will be commonplace. So consonant is this system with the nature of man that it is exactly parodied and profaned not only in the sailor's tavern, but in the Society ball. Here, for the lowest natures the result is drunkenness, disease and death; for the middle natures a gradual blunting of the finer feelings; for the higher, an exhilaration amounting at the best to the foundation of a life-long love. If these Society "rites" are properly performed, there should be no exhaustion. After a ball, one should feel the need of a long walk in the young morning air. The weariness or boredom, the headache or somnolence, are Nature's warnings.

VIII

Now the purpose of such a ball, the moral attitude on entering, seems to me to be of supreme importance. If you go with the idea of killing time, you are rather killing yourself. Baudelaire speaks of the first period of love when the boy kisses the trees of the wood, rather than kiss nothing. At the age of thirty-six I found myself at Pompeii, passionately kissing that great grave statue of a woman that stands in the avenue of the tombs. Even now, as I wake in the morning, I sometimes fall to kissing my own arms. It is with such a feeling that one should go to a ball, and with such a feeling intensified, purified and exalted, that one should leave it. If this be so, how much more if one go with the direct religious purpose burning in one's whole being!

Beethoven roaring at the sunrise is no strange spectacle to me, who shout with joy and wonder, when I understand (without which one cannot really be said ever to see) a blade of grass. I fall upon my knees in speechless adoration at the moon; I hide my eyes in holy awe from a good Van Gogh. Imagine then a ball in which the music is the choir celestial, the wine the wine of the Graal, or that of the Sabbath of the Adepts, and one's partner the Infinite and Eternal One, the True and Living God Most High! Go even to a common ball—the Moulin de la Galette will serve even the least of my magicians—with your whole soul aflame within you, and your whole will concentrated on these transubstantiations, and tell me what miracle takes place! It is the hate

205

of, the distaste for, life that sends one to the ball when one is old; when one is young one is on springs until the hour falls; but the love of God, which is the only true love, diminishes not with age; it grows deeper and intenser with every satisfaction. It seems as if in the noblest men this secretion constantly increases—which certainly suggests an external reservoir—so that age loses all its bitterness. We find "Brother Lawrence," Nicholas Herman of Lorraine, at the age of eighty in continuous enjoyment of union with God. Buddha at an equal age would run up and down the Eight High Trances like an acrobat on a ladder; stories not too dissimilar are told of Bishop Berkeley. Many persons have not attained union at all until middle age, and then have rarely lost it. It is true that genius in the ordinary sense of the word has nearly always showed itself in the young. Perhaps we should regard such cases as Nicholas Herman as cases of acquired genius. Now I am certainly of opinion that genius can be acquired, or, in the alternative, that it is an almost universal possession. Its rarity may be attributed to the crushing influence of a corrupted society. It is rare to meet a youth without high ideals, generous thoughts, a sense of holiness, of his own importance, which, being interpreted, is, of his own identity with God. Three years in the world, and he is a bank clerk or even a government official.

Only those who intuitively understand from early boyhood that they must stand out, and who have the incredible courage and endurance to do so in the face of all that tyranny, callousness, and the scorn of inferiors can do; only these arrive at manhood uncontaminated. Every serious or spiritual thought is made a jest; poets are thought "soft" and "cowardly," apparently because they are the only boys with a will of their own and courage to hold out against the whole school, boys and masters in league as once were Pilate and Herod; honour is replaced by expediency, holiness by hypocrisy. Even where we found thoroughly good seed sprouting in favourable ground, too often is there a frittering away of the forces. Facile encouragement of a poet or painter is far worse for him than any amount of opposition. Here again the sex question (S.Q. so-called by Tolstoyans, chastity-mongers, nut-fooders, and such who talk and think of nothing else) intrudes its horrid head. I believe that every boy is originally conscious of sex as sacred. But he does not know what it is. With infinite diffidence he asks. The master replies with holy horror; the boy with a low leer, a furtive laugh, perhaps worse. I am inclined to agree with the Head Master of Eton that pæderastic passions among schoolboys "do no harm"; further, I think them the only redeeming feature of sexual life at public schools. The Hindoos are wiser. At the well-watched hour of puberty the boy is prepared as for a sacrament; he is led to a duly consecrated temple, and there by a wise and holy woman, skilled in the art, and devoted to this end, he is initiated with all solemnity into the mystery of life. The act is thus declared religious, sacred, impersonal, utterly apart from amorism and eroticism and animalism and sentimentalism and all the other vilenesses that Protestantism has made of it. The Catholic Church did, I believe, to some extent preserve the Pagan tradition. Marriage is a sacrament. But in the attempt to deprive the act of all accretions which would profane it, the Fathers of the Church added in spite of themselves other accretions which profaned it more. They tied it to property and inheritance. They wished it to serve both God and Mammon. Rightly restraining the priest, who should employ his whole energy in the miracle of the Mass, they found their counsel a counsel of perfection. The magical tradition was in part lost; the priest could not do what was expected of him, and the unexpended portion of his energy turned sour. Hence the thoughts of priests, like the thoughts of modern faddists, revolved eternally around the S.Q. A special and secret Mass, a Mass of the Holy Ghost, a Mass of the Mystery of the Incarnation, to be performed at stated intervals, might have saved both monks and nuns, and given the Church eternal dominion of the world.

IX

To return. The rarity of genius is in great part due to the destruction of its young. Even as in physical life that is a favoured plant one of whose thousand seeds ever shoots forth a blade, so do conditions all but kill the strongest shoots of genius. But just as rabbits increased apace in Australia, where even a missionary has been known to beget ninety children in two years, so shall we be able to breed genius if we can find the conditions which hamper it, and remove them. The obvious practical step is to restore the rites of Bacchus, Aphrodite and Apollo to their proper place. They should not be open to every one, and manhood should be the reward of ordeal and initiation.

The physical tests should be severe, and weaklings should be killed out rather than artificially preserved. The same remark applies to intellectual tests. But such tests should be as wide as possible. I was an absolute duffer at school in all forms of athletics and games, because I despised them. I held, and still hold, numerous mountaineering world's records. Similarly, examinations fail to test intelligence. Cecil Rhodes refused to employ any man with a University degree. That such degrees lead to honour in England is a sign of England's decay, though even in England they are usually the stepping-stones to clerical idleness or pedagogic slavery. Such is a dotted outline of the picture that I wish to draw. If the power to possess property depended on a man's competence, and his perception of real values, a new aristocracy would at once be created, and the deadly fact that social consideration varies with the power of purchasing champagne would cease to be a fact. Our pluto-heiro-politicocracy would fall in a day. But I am only too well aware that such a picture is not likely to be painted. We can then only work patiently and in secret. We must select suitable material and train it in utmost reverence to these three master-methods, or aiding the soul in its genial orgasm.

<h1 style="text-align:center">X</h1>

This reverent attitude is of an importance which I cannot overrate. Normal people find normal relief from any general or special excitement in the sexual act. Commander Marston, R.N., whose experiments in the effect of the tom-tom on the married Englishwoman are classical and conclusive, has admirably described how the vague unrest which she at first shows gradually assumes the sexual form, and culminates, if allowed to do so, in shameless masturbation or indecent advances. But this is a natural corollary of the proposition that married Englishwomen are usually unacquainted with sexual satisfaction. Their desires are constantly stimulated by brutal and ignorant husbands, and never gratified. This fact again account for the amazing prevalence of Sapphism in London Society. The Hindus warn their pupils against the dangers of breathing exercises. Indeed the slightest laxness in moral or physical tissues may cause the energy accumulated by the practice to discharge itself by involuntary emission. I have known this happen in my own experience. It is then of the utmost importance to realize that the relief of tension is to be found in what the Hebrews and the Greeks called prophesying, and which is better when organized into art. The disorderly discharge is mere waste, a wilderness of howlings; the orderly discharge is a "Prometheus unbound," or "L'age d'airain," according to the special aptitudes of the enthused person. But it must be remembered the special aptitudes are very easy to acquire if the driving force of enthusiasm be great. If you cannot keep the rules of others, you make rules of your own. One set turns out in the long run to be just as good as the other. Henri Rousseau, the douanier, was laughed at all his life. I laughed as heartily as the rest; though, almost despite myself, I kept on saying (as the phrase goes) "that I felt something; couldn't say what." The moment it occurred to somebody to put up all his paintings in one room by themselves, it was instantly apparent that his naïveté was the simplicity of a Master. Let no one then imagine that I fail to perceive or underestimate the dangers of employing these methods. The occurrence even of so simple a matter as fatigue might change a Las Meninas into a stupid sexual crisis. It will be necessary for most Englishmen to emulate the self-control of the Arabs and Hindus, whose ideal is to deflower the greatest possible number of virgins—eighty is considered a fairly good performance—without completing the act. It is, indeed, of the first importance for the celebrant in any phallic rite to be able to complete the act without even once allowing a sexual or sensual thought to invade his mind. The mind must be as absolutely detached from one's own body as it is from another person's.

XI

Of musical instruments few are suitable. The human voice is the best, and the only one which can be usefully employed in chorus. Anything like an orchestra implies infinite rehearsal, and introduces an atmosphere of artificiality. The organ is a worthy solo instrument, and is an orchestra in itself, while its tone and associations favour the religious idea. The violin is the most useful of all, for its every mood expresses the hunger for the infinite, and yet it is so mobile that it has a greater emotional range than any of its competitors. Accompaniment must be dispensed with, unless a harpist be available. The harmonium is a horrible instrument, if only because of its associations; and the piano is like unto it, although, if unseen and played by a

Paderewski, it would serve. The trumpet and the bell are excellent, to startle, and the crises of a ceremony. Hot, drubbing, passionate, in a different class of ceremony, a class more intense and direct, but on the whole less exalted, the tom-tom stands alone. It combines well with the practice of mantra, and is the best accompaniment for any sacred dance.

XII

Of sacred dances the most practical for a gathering is the seated dance. One sits cross-legged on the floor, and sways two and fro from the hips in time with the mantra. A solo or duet of dancers as a spectacle rather distracts from this exercise. I would suggest a very small and very brilliant light on the floor in the middle of the room. Such a room is best floored with mosaic marble; an ordinary Freemason's Lodge carpet is not a bad thing. The eyes, if they see anything at all, see then only the rhythmical or mechanical squares leading in perspective to the simple unwinking light. The swinging of the body with the mantra (which has a habit of rising and falling as if of its own accord in a very weird way) becomes more accentuated; ultimately a curiously spasmodic stage occurs, and then the consciousness flickers and goes out; perhaps breaks through into the divine consciousness, perhaps is merely recalled to itself by some variable in external impression. The above is a very simple description of a very simple and earnest form of ceremony, based entirely upon rhythm. It is very easy to prepare, and its results are usually very encouraging for the beginner.

XIII

Wine being a mocker and strong drink raging, its use is more likely to lead to trouble than mere music. One essential difficulty is dosage. One certainly needs enough; and, as Blake points out, one can only tell what is enough by taking too much. For each man the dose varies enormously; so does it for the same man at different times. The ceremonial escape from this is to have a noiseless attendant to bear the bowl of libation, and present it to each in turn, at frequent intervals. Small doses should be drunk, and the bowl passed on, taken as the worshipper deems advisable. Yet the cup-bearer should be an initiate, and use his own discretion before presenting the bowl. The slightest sign that intoxication is mastering the man should be a sign to him to pass that man. This practice can be easily fitted to the ceremony previously described. If desired, instead of wine, the elixir introduced by me to Europe may be employed. But its results, if used in this way, have not as yet been thoroughly studied. It is my immediate purpose to repair this neglect.

XIV

The sexual excitement, which must complete the harmony of method, offers a more difficult problem. It is exceptionally desirable that the actual bodily movements involved should be decorous in the highest sense, and many people are so ill-trained that they will be unable to regard such a ceremony with any but critical or lascivious eyes; either would be fatal to all the good already done. It is presumably better to wait until all present are greatly exalted before risking a profanation. It is not desirable, in my opinion, that the ordinary worshippers should celebrate in public. The sacrifice should be single. Whether or no . . .

XV

Thus far had I written when the distinguished poet, whose conversation with me upon the Mysteries had incited me to jot down these few rough notes, knocked at my door. I told him that I was at work on the ideas suggested by him, and that—well, I was rather stuck. He asked permission to glance at the MS. (For he reads English fluently, though speaking but a few words), and having done so, kindled and said: "If you come with me now, we will finish your essay." Glad enough of any excuse to stop working, the more plausible the better, I hastened to take down my coat and hat. "By the way," he remarked in the automobile, "I take it that you do not mind giving me the Word of Rose Croix." Surprised, I exchanged the secrets of I.N.R.I. with him. "And now, very excellent and perfect Prince," he said, "what follows is under this seal." And he gave me the most solemn of all Masonic tokens. "You are about," said he, "to compare your ideal with our real." He touched a bell. The automobile stopped, and we got out. He

211

dismissed the chauffeur. "Come," he said, "we have a brisk half-mile." We walked through thick woods to an old house, where we were greeted in silence by a gentleman who, though in court dress, wore a very "practicable" sword. On satisfying him, we were passed through a corridor to an anteroom, where another armed guardian awaited us. He, after a further examination, proceeded to offer me a court dress, the insignia of a Sovereign Prince of Rose Croix, and a garter and mantle, the former of green silk, the latter of green velvet, and lined with cerise silk. "It is a low mass," whispered the guardian. In this anteroom were three or four others, both ladies and gentlemen, busily robing. In a third room we found a procession formed, and joined it. There were twenty-six of us in all. Passing a final guardian we reached the chapel itself, at whose entrance stood a young man and a young woman, both dressed in simple robes of white silk embroidered with gold, red and blue. The former bore a torch of resinous wood, the latter sprayed us as we passed with attar of roses from a cup. The room in which we now were had at one time been a chapel; so much its shape declared. But the high altar was covered with a cloth that displayed the Rose and Cross, while above it were ranged seven candelabra, each of seven branches. The stalls had been retained; and at each knight's hand burned a taper of rose-coloured wax, and a bouquet of roses was before him. In the centre of the nave was a great cross—a "calvary cross of ten squares," measuring, say, six feet by five—painted in red upon a white board, at whose edges were rings through which passed gilt staves. At each corner was a banner, bearing lion, bull, eagle and man, and from the top of their staves sprang a canopy of blue, wherein were figured in gold the twelve emblems of the Zodiac. Knights and Dames being installed, suddenly a bell tinkled in the architrave. Instantly all rose. The doors opened at a trumpet peal from without, and a herald advanced, followed by the High Priest and Priestess. The High Priest was a man of nearly sixty years, if I may judge by the white beard; but he walked with the springy yet assured step of the thirties. The High Priestess, a proud, tall, sombre woman of perhaps thirty summers, walked by his side, their hands raised and touching as in the minuet. Their trains were borne by the two youths who had admitted us. All this while an unseen organ played an introit. This ceased as they took their places at the altar. They faced West, waiting. On the closing of the doors the armed guard, who was clothed in a scarlet robe instead of green, drew his sword, and went up and down the aisle, chanting exorcisms and swinging the great sword. All present drew their swords and faced outward, holding the points in front of them. This part of the ceremony appeared interminable. When it was over the girl and boy reappeared; bearing, the one a bowl, the other a censer. Singing some litany or other, apparently in Greek, though I could not catch the words, they purified and consecrated the chapel.

Now the High Priest and High Priestess began a litany in rhythmic lines of equal length. At each third response they touched hands in a peculiar manner; at each seventh they kissed. The twenty-first was a complete embrace. The bell tinkled in the architrave; and they parted. The High Priest then took from the altar a flask curiously shaped to imitate a phallus. The High Priestess knelt and presented a boat-shaped cup of gold. He knelt opposite her, and did not pour from the flask. Now the Knights and Dames began a long litany; first a Dame in treble, then a Knight in bass, then a response in chorus of all present with the organ. This Chorus was: EVOE HO, IACCHE! EPELTHON, EPELTHON, EVOE, IAO!

Again and again it rose and fell. Towards its close, whether by "stage effect" or no I could not swear, the light over the altar grew rosy, then purple. The High Priest sharply and suddenly threw up his hand; instant silence. He now poured out the wine from the flask. The High Priestess gave it to the girl attendant, who bore it to all present. This was no ordinary wine. It has been said of vodki that it looks like water and tastes like fire. With this wine the reverse is the case. It was of a rich fiery gold in which flames of light danced and shook, but its taste was limpid and pure like fresh spring water. No sooner had I drunk of it, however, than I began to tremble. It was a most astonishing sensation; I can imagine a man feel thus as he awaits his executioner, when he has passed through fear, and is all excitement. I looked down my stall, and saw that each was similarly affected. During the libation the High Priestess sang a hymn, again in Greek. This time I recognized the words; they were those of an ancient Ode to Aphrodite. The boy attendant now descended to the red cross, stooped and kissed it; then he danced upon it in such a way that he seemed to be tracing the patterns of a marvellous rose of gold, for the percussion caused a shower of bright dust to fall from the canopy.

Meanwhile the litany (different words, but the same chorus) began again. This time it was a duet between the High Priest and Priestess. At each chorus Knights and Dames bowed low. The girl moved round continuously, and the bowl passed. This ended in the exhaustion of the boy, who fell fainting on the cross. The girl immediately took the bowl and put it to his lips. Then she raised him, and, with the assistance of the Guardian of the Sanctuary, led him out of the chapel. The bell again tinkled in the architrave. The herald blew a fanfare. The High Priest and High Priestess moved stately to each other and embraced, in the act unloosing the heavy golden robes which they wore. These fell, twin lakes of gold. I now saw her dressed in a garment of white watered silk, lined throughout (as it appeared later) with ermine. The High Priest's vestment was an elaborate embroidery of every colour, harmonized by exquisite yet robust art. He wore also a breastplate corresponding to the canopy; a sculptured "beast" at each corner in gold, while the twelve signs of the Zodiac were symbolized by the stones of the breastplate. The bell tinkled yet again, and the herald again sounded his trumpet. The celebrants moved hand in hand down the nave while the organ thundered forth its solemn harmonies. All the Knights and Dames rose and gave the secret sign of the Rose Croix. It was at this part of the ceremony that things began to happen to me. I became suddenly aware that my body had lost both weight and tactile sensibility. My consciousness seemed to be situated no longer in my body. I "mistook myself," if I may use the phrase, for one of the stars in the canopy. In this way I missed seeing the celebrants actually approach the cross. The bell tinkled again; I came back to myself, and then I saw that the High Priestess, standing at the foot of the cross, had thrown her robe over it so that the cross was no longer visible. There was only a board covered with ermine. She was now naked but for her coloured and jewelled head-dress and the heavy torque of gold about her neck, and the armlets and anklets that matched it. She began to sing in a soft strange tongue, so low and smoothly that in my partial bewilderment I could not hear at all; but I caught a few words, Io Paian! Io Pan! and a phrase in which the words Iao Sabao ended emphatically a sentence in which I caught the words Eros, Thelema and Sebazo. While she did this she unloosed the breastplate and gave it to the girl

214

attendant. The robe followed; I saw that they were naked and unashamed. For the first time there was absolute silence. Now, from an hundred jets surrounding the board poured forth a perfumed purple smoke. The world was wrapt in a fond gauze of mist, sacred as the clouds upon the mountains. Then at a signal given by the High Priest, the bell tinkled once more. The celebrants stretched out their arms in the form of a cross, interlacing their fingers. Slowly they revolved through three circles and a half. She then laid him down upon the cross, and took her own appointed place. The organ now again rolled forth its solemn music. I was lost to everything. Only this I saw, that the celebrants made no expected motion. The movements were extremely small and yet extremely strong.

This must have continued for a great length of time. To me it seemed as if eternity itself could not contain the variety and depth of my experiences. Tongue nor pen could record them; and yet I am fain to attempt the impossible. 1. I was, certainly and undoubtedly, the star in the canopy. This star was an incomprehensibly enormous world of pure flame. 2. I suddenly realized that the star was of no size whatever. It was not that the star shrank, but that it (=I) became suddenly conscious of infinite space. 3. An explosion took place. I was in consequence a point of light, infinitely small, yet infinitely bright, and this point was without position. 4. Consequently this point was ubiquitous, and there was a feeling of infinite bewilderment, blinded after a very long time by a gust of infinite rapture (I use the word "blinded" as if under constraint; I should have preferred to use the words "blotted out" or "overwhelmed" or "illuminated"). 5. This infinite fullness—I have not described it as such, but it was that—was suddenly changed into a feeling of infinite emptiness, which became conscious as a yearning. 6. These two feelings began to alternate, always with suddenness, and without in any way overlapping, with great rapidity. 7. This alternation must have occurred fifty times—I had rather have said an hundred. 8. The two feelings suddenly became one. Again the word explosion is the only one that gives any idea of it. 9. I now seemed to be conscious of everything at once, that it was at the same time one and many. I say "at once," that is, I was not successively all things, but instantaneously. 10. This being, if I may call it being, seemed to drop into an infinite abyss of Nothing. 11. While this "falling" lasted, the bell suddenly tinkled three times. I instantly became my normal self, yet with a constant awareness, which has never left me to this hour, that the truth of the matter is not this normal "I" but "That" which is still dropping into Nothing. I am assured by those who know that I may be able to take up the thread if I attend another ceremony.

The tinkle died away. The girl attendant ran quickly forward and folded the ermine over the celebrants. The herald blew a fanfare, and the Knights and Dames left their stalls. Advancing to the board, we took hold of the gilded carrying poles, and followed the herald in procession out of the chapel, bearing the litter to a small side-chapel leading out of the middle anteroom, where we left it, the guard closing the doors. In silence we disrobed, and left the house. About a mile through the woods we found my friend's automobile waiting. I asked him, if that was a low mass, might I not be permitted to witness a High Mass? "Perhaps," he answered with a curious smile, "if all they tell of you is true." In the meantime he permitted me to describe the ceremony and its results as faithfully as I was able, charging me only to give no indication of the city near which it took place. I am willing to indicate to initiates of the Rose Croix degree of Masonry under proper charter from the genuine authorities (for there are spurious Masons working under a forged charter) the address of a person willing to consider their fitness to affiliate to a Chapter practicing similar rites.

XVI

I consider it supererogatory to continue my essay on the Mysteries and my analysis of Energized Enthusiasm.

With regard to the article in No. 9, "Energized Enthusiasm," a circumstance of exceptional interest has arisen. The author was not acquainted at that time with the literature of those gnostics who were the earliest and only true Christians. In Fragments of a Faith Forgotten, however, we find the following passage: "After the banquet they keep the holy all-night festival. And this is how it is kept. They all stand up in a body, and about the middle of the entertainment they first of all separate into two bands, men in one and

216

women in the other. And a leader is chosen for each, the conductor whose reputation is greatest and the one most suitable for the post. They then chant hymns made in God's honour in many metres and melodies, sometimes singing in chorus, sometimes one band beating time to the answering chant of the other, (now) dancing to its music, (now) inspiring it, at one time in processional hymns, at another in standing songs, turning and re-turning in the dance.

"Then when each band has feasted (that is, has sung and danced) apart by itself, drinking of God-pleasing (nectar), just as in the Bacchic rites men drink the wine unmixed, then they join together and one chorus is formed of the two bands, in imitation of the joined chorus on the banks of the Red Sea, because of the wonderful works that had been there wrought. For the sea at God's command became for one party a cause of safety and for the other a cause of ruin.

"So the chorus of men and women Therapeuts, being formed as closely as possible on this model, by means of melodies in parts and harmony—the high notes of the women answering to the deep tones of the men—produces a harmonious and most musical symphony. The ideas are of the most beautiful, the expressions of the most beautiful, and the dancers reverent; while the goal of the ideas, expressions, and dances is piety.

"Thus drunken unto morning's light with this fair drunkenness, with no head-heaviness or drowsiness, but with eyes and body fresher even than when they came to the banquet, they take their stand at dawn, when, catching sight of the rising sun, they raise their hands to heaven, praying for sunlight and truth and keenness of spiritual vision. After this prayer each returns to his own sanctuary, to his accustomed traffic in philosophy and labour in its fields.

"So far then about the Therapeuts, who are devoted to the contemplation of nature and live in it and in the soul alone, citizens of heaven and the world, legitimately recommended to the Father and Creator of the Universe by their virtue, which procures them His love, virtue that sets before it for its prize the most suitable reward of nobility and goodness, outstripping every gift of fortune and the first comer in the race to the very goal of blessedness."

The striking identity of this with the account of the ritual derived from a priori considerations will at once be manifest.

Colophon

Neophyte Libri: Official Neophyte Reading
Syllabus

This volume was compiled from public domain
sources and prepared for publication by Frater
Lachesis Peyton.

Published by Saklas Publishing
2025

V

A∴A∴

www.ingramcontent.com/pod-product-compliance
Lightning Source LLC
Chambersburg PA
CBHW021138130626
46554CB00005B/1556